To Harry Robinson,

who championed evangelism in the Anglican Church of Canada long before it was popular to do so, and who made the path much easier for those of us who follow, whose ministry has been an exemplary model of evangelism through congregational life, and who has had a greater influence on my life and ministry than he knows or I can say.

Good News People

An Introduction to Evangelism for Tongue-Tied Christians

Harold Percy

with a Study Guide by
Michael Knowles

Anglican Book Centre
Toronto, Canada

1996
Anglican Book Centre
600 Jarvis Street
Toronto, Ontario
M4Y 2J6

All biblical quotations are from the *New Revised Standard Version Bible*, copyright © 1989, by the Division of Christian Education of the National Council of the Churches of Christ in the United States of America. Used by permission.

For a fuller treatment of the issues discussed in Chapter 4, including the story of the spies, see chapter 3 of Donald Posterski, *Reinventing Evangelism* (Markham, Ont: IVP, 1989).

Canadian Cataloguing in Publication Data

Percy, Harold.
  Good news people

ISBN 1–55126–165–0

1. Evangelistic work.   2. Anglican Church of Canada.
I. Knowles, Michael, 1956–   .   II. Title.

BV3790.P47 1996   269'.2   C96–931673–9

Contents

Foreword

The Decade of Evangelism is well past its midpoint, and proponents and skeptics alike are already beginning to assess its significance for the church in the 90s. Superficially it will be easy to criticize, as most churches fail to attract new members in great numbers. Those who counted on the Decade to solve their financial problems by adding large numbers of converts to their rolls will doubtless be disappointed. Others who were once wary of popular evangelistic enterprises will be confirmed in their pessimism, not that much long-term comfort can be derived by such negativism.

Those who are prepared to look more closely, however, will find important signs of hope, and will celebrate the Decade as a possible turning point for the church's self-understanding of its mission. A number of these signs are illuminated by the work of the Rev. Harold Percy. A parish priest of the Anglican Church of Canada, Percy is the founding director of the Wycliffe College Institute of Evangelism. In that capacity he maintains a daunting schedule of lecturing, offering seminars across Canada, and mentoring students and clergy, all the while leading a growing parish in a Toronto suburb.

In the midst of these responsibilities, Harold Percy produces a steady stream of articles, newspaper columns, and now a second book, *Good News People*. This is a book for ordinary Christians — lay people and clergy — who are looking for a clear, straightforward rationale for the work of evangelism in the church today. With charity, humour, and decisiveness, Percy tackles many of the objections raised to much that passes for evangelism today. His thesis is that, through the life, witness, death and resurrection of Jesus Christ, God has acted to rescue and renew the world.

It is the mission of the church to proclaim that good news and — equally important — to model the kind of community that faith in Jesus ought to produce. In an earlier age, when society seemed to possess a veneer of Christianity, the church understood its vocation to function as a centre for pastoral care of the faithful. Without denying the continuing importance of Christian care, Percy insists that the church must shift to a model of disciple making; and that means evangelism.

In a society that promotes specialization in all sorts of endeavours, it is not surprising that the church will expect evangelism to be done by its own cadre of experts. While recognizing the special ministry of individual evangelists, Percy places primary responsibility for evangelism at the door of the church itself. The church is the evangelizing community; that is its nature; that must become its first calling. At first this feels threatening — if I cannot any longer count on someone else to evangelize, then I must redefine or rediscover my own vocation as a member of an evangelizing community. So with patience and clarity, Harold Percy disarms the fears of reluctant would-be evangelists, and shows us how we can begin moulding and telling our own Christian story so that others may hear, receive, and respond to it.

As the Decade of Evanglism moves to its closing years, some churches will continue to decline. Others will find new, effective ways forward in refocussing their sense of call. *Good News People* will help many of those churches which study, absorb, pray, and implement Harold Percy's vision.

Peter Mason,
Bishop of the Diocese of Ontario

Introduction

At the Lambeth Conference of 1988, the bishops of the Worldwide Anglican Communion passed a resolution calling for the 1990s to be a Decade of Evangelism. Many of the churches in the developing world greeted this resolution with rejoicing, but it is fair to say that in the churches of the West, it received a decidedly mixed reaction.

In Canada, one of the major tasks during the first half of the decade has been to reclaim the word "evangelism," to rescue it from the bad reputation it has suffered in recent decades, to rid it of many of the negative stereotypes it has acquired in our culture, and to convince Anglicans — laity and clergy alike — that this is a ministry the Church should be proud to claim, that belongs at the top of the Church's agenda.

Thank God, this is happening! At the beginning of the decade, one of the most frequently heard questions was "Why should we want to get involved in evangelism?" Halfway through the decade that question was largely replaced by the much more positive "How can we do evangelism effectively and with integrity?" This is great progress indeed!

This book is intended for "ordinary" mainline Christians (perhaps particularly, but certainly not exclusively, Anglicans) who want to know more about evangelism. It addresses the basic questions of what it is, why it is important, and how local congregations and individual Christians can share in this important and joyful ministry.

In *The Renewal of Anglicanism*, Alistair McGrath writes,

> There is something intrinsically attractive about the Christian faith and, supremely, about the person of Jesus Christ. It is like a "pearl of great price," — something that is

recognized to be worth seeking and possessing, and whose possession overshadows everything else. The fundamental motivation for evangelism is generosity — the basic human concern to share the good things of life with those whom we love. It does not reflect a desire to sell or dominate; it arises from love and compassion on the part of those who have found something wonderful and want others to share in its joy. It is, as the old adage has it, like one beggar telling another where to find bread (p. 53).

Exactly. A local church that is helping people come to a convinced and intentional faith in Jesus Christ and to grow towards maturity in that faith is a magnetic church. To be part of such a church is a joy. To be a part of the process through which a person comes to a vibrant and living faith in Jesus Christ is sheer exhilaration. I pray for every person who reads this book, and every congregation they represent, that they might know this joy. May this book help you and your parish become more confident, more excited, and more effective in sharing the good news about Jesus, and may you find great joy in return! In this lies the key to the renewal of our congregations and of our Church.

Harold Percy
Trinity Anglican Church
Streetsville, Ontario

CHAPTER ONE

What's All the Fuss?

The cartoon showed a well-dressed woman speaking to her rector on her way out of church. "What's all this fuss about evangelism?" she asked him. "Surely everyone in this town who ought to be an Anglican already is one."

Many people in the Church are genuinely puzzled about the recent emphasis on evangelism. They find themselves wondering why the issue has suddenly become so important. The truth is that evangelism hasn't suddenly become an important issue. It has always been important. Evangelism was the heartbeat of the New Testament church.

The sad truth is that this important ministry has suffered from a long period of neglect in many churches. To the degree that this is so, it is fair to say that the Church has lost its way and forgotten what it is about. Passion for evangelism is a key indicator of faithfulness for the Church. A lack of interest in evangelism is both a cause and a result of the malaise that currently characterizes many churches.

The church is called to many important and legitimate expressions of ministry, but evangelism is always at its heart, and when evangelism is neglected, the Church will always be much less than God calls it to be. Evangelism is important to the Church, because the world is important to God.

Good News for a Hurting World

It doesn't take great insight to realize that we live in a hurting world. Morning after morning the daily news-paper at our doorstep chronicles the latest instalment in the tale of the world's misery. There are stories of war and famine and every form of tragedy imaginable. There are stories of sickness and cruelty, of crime and domestic violence. Page after page, it goes on and on. In our own neighbourhoods and families, we are aware of deep suffering and fear. Life is beautiful in many ways, but there is no denying that this world is racked with pain.

The Gospel is God's response to this pain. The Good News is about God's inexhaustible love for this world and the initiative God has taken in the life, death, and resurrection of Jesus to heal us, to rescue us all from the power of evil, and to heal us of its wounds and scars. In evangelism, we are called to share this Gospel — which means, literally, "Good News." Evangelism takes place where God's heart and human need meet; it takes place when God's people understand that they have been given this ministry of reconciliation and hope — that they are called to be a Good News People.

Human Need

People Are Lost

In the nineteenth chapter of Luke's Gospel we read the story of the tax collector Zacchaeus. This story was a favourite of mine as a child because I was fascinated with the idea of a grown man climbing a tree! Because he was a tax collector, taking money in the name of the heathen Roman occupying power, we can safely assume two things about Zacchaeus. First of all, he was extremely affluent. Secondly, he was despised by his fellow citizens in Jericho. When Zacchaeus took Jesus home for dinner that evening, we can be reasonably certain that Jesus was going into a very fine house. The signs of wealth and success would have been all around. The people of Jericho, commenting on the comfortable lifestyle that Zacchaeus enjoyed at their expense, would have used many colourful words to describe the way they felt about him. But none of them would have thought to use the word that Jesus used.

Jesus said that Zacchaeus was *lost*. Then, rejoicing in Zaccheus's change of heart, Jesus said, "Today salvation has come to this house, because this man, too, is a son of Abraham. For the Son of Man came to seek and to save what was lost" (Luke 19:9–10).

There are people all around us, in our places of work, in the neighbourhoods where we live, who are just like Zacchaeus. Outwardly, they appear to have it all together. They are pleasant, urbane, sophisticated, educated, affluent. But inwardly, they are aware of a gnawing hunger for a deeper reality. Who in Jericho would ever have guessed that Zacchaeus was spiritually hungry? Would he ever have let his guard down long enough to let anyone get even a hint of his inner longing? Yet there he was, desperate enough to climb a tree, just to get a glimpse of Jesus!

We should not be deceived by appearances. We are all products of a society that has mastered the art of projecting the proper image. We are incredibly skilled at this. People know how to live without ever letting on what questions, doubts, fears, and emptiness are churning just below the surface. We even know how to fool ourselves much of the time! As people who are beginning to think seriously about evangelism, we need to remember that we are surrounded by lost, needy people who are hungering for spiritual depth and reality.

Baptist preacher and sociologist Tony Campolo has an intriguing lecture called "Who Switched the Price Tags?" He begins by asking us to imagine a department store that someone enters at night, to switch the price tags around. The tags from the cheap goods in the bargain basement are taken upstairs and put on articles of great value. The high price tags from the valuable goods are taken downstairs and put on the cheap items. Imagine the confusion that would arise when the store opened for business the next morning.

The point of the lecture is that something like this has happened in life. The articles of great value have been marked way down, while articles of lesser value have been grossly inflated. Our loving relationships, our children, our spiritual lives, our appreciation of the beauty of nature, and our health are neglected while we pursue worldly success and financial gain.

I read a graphic but rather tragic phrase a while ago. Referring to the emptiness of people who have risen to the top of their fields but have failed to find happiness, the writer said, "Many people spend their whole lives struggling to get to the top of the ladder, only to discover at the top that it is leaning against the wrong wall." It is so easy in this life to lose our way — to spend all our energy going top speed in the wrong direction or meandering along endless byways that lead nowhere.

I love watching track events in the various national and international competitions we see on television. Athletes with magnificently tuned bodies race down the track, every muscle straining, then explode across the finish line. I love the little ritual the winner performs: a swaggering little jaunt in front of the grandstand to receive the adulation of the crowd, one arm high in the air and one finger pointing to the sky, proclaiming proudly, "I am number one!"

Imagine, as this ritual is being performed, that the final athlete in the race comes struggling down the track. The race is long over, but here comes the final contestant, far behind. Imagine what might happen if the judges were to come out of their box, point to this latecomer, and announce, "The winner!" Imagine that they then turn to the front runner, who is still doing his little victory dance, and say, "Last!" There would be confusion all over the place. The athletes would argue and protest; the spectators would boo in anger and bewilderment. They'd look at each other and say, "What's going on?" Imagine the judge explaining: "Oh, did you think this event was about speed? Who ever told you such a thing? You've been deceived. It's about form. That runner up front was going far too fast; there's no way he could have paid proper attention to form. The slower runner did it right. He took his time and paid attention to good style."

The scenario is preposterous. Yet this is precisely what happens in life. We have been told lies. We have been told that life is about getting ahead, about making money, about accumulating possessions — about being successful. We have been told that our value lies in our ability to purchase and that we are measured by what we own. We have been led to believe that we must serve only our own interests so we will get our "rightful share" of the pie. People work themselves into exhaustion in the service of these lies. Along the way, things of far greater value are often neglected.

In the four New Testament Gospels, we find Jesus, again and again, using an intriguing phrase. After telling a story or making some point in a discussion, he sometimes adds, almost as an afterthought: "The first will be last, and the last will be first." People must have gone home scratching their heads and wondering what on earth such gibberish could mean. Why ruin a great story with a line like that?

Taken in its historical context, of course, Jesus was warning the leaders of Israel not to presume too heavily upon their status as the chosen nation through which God would be disclosed to the world. But the line has a more universal application, which is equally valid. It is quite simply true that because of the lies we have been fed about the meaning of life, many people who by the standards of this world are declared to be winners are, by the standards of God's reign, losers. They are, in fact, lost. The deceptive voices of this age are all around us, singing their seductive songs, enticing us, lulling us into forgetting who we are, encouraging us to go a different way from the one we were created for. We are surrounded by people who, despite appearances to the contrary, are lost. They need help finding their way, just as we need help in finding our way. We need help in learning how to live. Evangelism is important because it offers help to people who have lost their way.

People Yearn for Wholeness

As a preacher and Christian communicator, I regularly make a point of browsing around in popular bookstores to see what people are reading. When I come to the "Self-Help" section of the store, I never fail to be amazed. The production of self-help books has to be one of the greatest financial success stories of our time! Month after month, new titles appear in a never-ending stream, and the market for this material is huge. The cover blurbs trumpet sales in terms of millions, not thousands, of copies. The range of topics the material covers is equally breathtaking. There are books on how to be more assertive in order to get what you want, how to be better organized or disciplined, and how to be more successful in your career. You can learn how to figure out your spouse, how to improve communication in your marriage, and how to become a better sexual performer and enjoy yourself more in the process. Other books promise to help you become more likeable, and show you how to develop more meaningful relationships. Still others promise help with the healing of hurts from childhood years, with rising above resentment, and with overcoming various forms of addiction and character weakness. Much of this material is no doubt very good and helpful, and some of it is probably not much good at all. I will leave that for others to judge. My point here is simply that the sheer magnitude of this growing body of material, and its warm reception in the marketplace, is evidence of a widespread and deep-seated yearning for wholeness.

This yearning for wholeness and healing is further evidenced by the popularity of self-help groups. Like the written material, these groups are growing rapidly, and they cover a wide range of topics. They meet in church halls, local recreation centres, individual homes, and private rooms in restaurants and hotels. In these groups, people meet to help one another deal with a wide range of issues, from addiction and codependence to wounds and scars they have received through many forms of victimization and abuse.

Addiction and abuse are the scourges of contemporary society. What is it about modern life that makes people so prone to addiction? Some time ago I read an interview in the newspaper with a television performer who asked, "If money is able to make people happy, why are so many rich people snuffing cocaine up their noses?" In most communities of any significant size, support and self-help will be available to help people deal with addictions to such things as alcohol, drugs, sex, gambling, shopping, and eating. The twelve-step program, originally developed for Alcoholics Anonymous, has been adapted to deal with a wide range of addictions, and the number of twelve-step groups across the country is increasing daily.

We are also becoming more and more aware of the high incidence of abusive behaviour going on behind closed doors and in secret places. In many of our communities, there is a need for hostels that provide shelter and protection for women who are beaten by their husbands. As a parish priest, I have heard some of their stories. Frequently, the victims of this domestic violence have to continue to live in fear while they wait for an opportunity to escape from their homes. With their bewildered children in tow and only the personal belongings they can carry in one or two bags, they make their way to the hostel, trembling with fear and shame.

We hear harrowing stories of children who have been sexually abused by an adult in a position of trust, or who have been preyed upon by a stranger in a public place. Increasingly, adults are coming forward with accusations that they were molested in childhood and would now like to get some help in dealing with the wounds they have been carrying down through the years. The road to recovery here is often long and arduous.

This is the social context in which we are called to carry out the ministry of evangelism. Many people are desperately hoping to hear some good news. As we walk along the streets of our cities and towns, we need to be constantly reminding ourselves that, all around us, people of all ages and from all walks of life are searching for wholeness and healing. We have to ask ourselves what Jesus might feel like in this particular situation, and what needs he might see.

We cannot afford to be simplistic, nor can we minimize the damage that many people have suffered or the difficulty of their healing process. Instead we are called to share humbly what God has done for this broken world, and for all its hurting inhabitants, through the death and resurrection of Jesus Christ. In the midst of sickness and pain, God wants the Church — the community of people who are committed to Jesus and who are learning what it means to follow Him — to be Good News People.

People Are Lonely

As Henry David Thoreau once said, many people are living lives of quiet desperation. Some are suffering from acute loneliness. I am convinced that loneliness is one of the greatest problems of our time. The fast pace and the competitive nature of modern life make this almost inevitable. For many people, the most appropriate lifestyle symbol would be the expressway. Life has become a mad rush from one activity or responsibility to the next. All around me, I see people who are totally exhausted. It is difficult to initiate and nurture deep, caring relationships and genuine intimacy when life is one big rush.

For other people, the most appropriate symbol for life is the ladder. Life is about climbing higher and higher, always struggling to make it to the top. But ladders are lonely places. You stand on each rung by yourself. If you are racing against other people to get to the top, the ladder can be painful and dangerous as well. There is always someone trying to pull you down or fighting to keep you from passing them. When our workplaces become places of heated competition, we can never really relax and develop friendships. Our fellow workers become our competitors! So we can't afford to drop our guard, to admit any need, to show any weakness or inadequacy. We need to develop a false front!

The same goes on in many neighbourhoods, where people compete to have the most attractive house, the sleekest car, the best vacation, the smartest, highest-performing children. So much of our modern lifestyle is affected by an undercurrent of competition and rivalry. Even where this competition is not so obvious, the busyness of life often means that our residential neighbourhoods are not really communities of friends, but simply collections of dormitories, whose inhabitants are strangers to one another.

The stresses and pressures of modern life make it more and more difficult to sustain intimate relationships. The high incidence of marriage breakdown hardly needs commentary. It is worth noting, however, that this is just the tip of the iceberg. Not every marriage that remains intact is healthy. Many people choose not to separate for various reasons but are aware that their relationship lacks true intimacy and companionship. Loneliness does not simply mean being alone. Many people living in intact family situations are suffering from acute loneliness. My purpose here is not to attempt a solution to this problem. It is merely to remind us, as we think about evangelism, that we should not be deceived by appearances. Many lonely people wish they could hear some good news.

People Need Hope

In the course of our daily activities, we meet a lot of people who are wondering whether life can possibly have any meaning at all. Is there any grand design to life, any goal or purpose to history, or is life just one thing after another, some good, some bad, hopefully with a few breaks along the way, perhaps a few highlights and a bit of excitement or pleasure, and then, at some point, death? In the human heart there is a desire for significance. We want to know that our lives have some meaning. Loren Mead of the Alban Institute writes, in *The Once and Future Church*, that it is the tension between meaning and meaninglessness "that is the driving power of history, not the minor . . . [tension between] communism and capitalism that political economists have argued for the past century and a half" (p. 85).

We want to know that what we do and how we live, somewhere, somehow, matters. Many people find that the common answers they are given — that life is about being successful or about being happy — do not suffice. They yearn for a connection with some form of transcendence. They can't escape the sense that their lives should be part of something much bigger, much grander than they have experienced so far. In the face of even their best accomplishments or during their moments of deepest joy, they find themselves wondering what it all ultimately means.

Again, it is important to remind ourselves that it is in such a context of wondering, searching, wrestling, and questioning that the ministry of evangelism is carried on. There are many searching hearts in which the Good News, sensitively shared, will find fertile soil.

People Need Forgiveness

Many people are going through life with an uneasy conscience. Others have deep regrets that dog their lives every step of the way. Some have acted dishonestly or violently and they are ashamed of themselves. Some have violated vows of fidelity and caused deep pain. Some have done things for which they believe they could never be forgiven. The fact that our modern age has almost lost a sense of sin or guilt does little to help these people. It only makes it more difficult for them to find the correct words and categories to express their need. But all around us are people in all walks of life who would like to have some stain or regret taken away, who would like to begin again, with a fresh page. People thinking about evangelism need to be aware of the fact that there are depths of guilt, regret, and remorse in the hearts of many people, and that the Gospel speaks directly to such situations.

People Are Afraid of Death

I once heard a preacher ask the congregation to imagine that we had all been invited on a cruise. The scenario went like this: At the beginning of the cruise, the captain comes down to speak to the passengers. He describes the ship and all the available activities. There will be wonderful meals, he says, with all the food you want; there will be sporting activities; and there is a library, a theatre, and a gymnasium. Every night a band will play in the ballroom and the dancing will go on until the early hours of morning. It's all there for the taking. The captain tells everyone to enjoy themselves — but then adds that there's one more thing of which everyone should be aware. Before the ship returns to port, he says, it's going to sink, and everyone will drown. But don't let that bother you, he says. Just put it out of your minds and have a good time!

Well, we might be able to do that for small stretches of time, occasionally. But inevitably, during the cruise, the thought of the ship's fate will force itself into our minds. Just when we are enjoying the gourmet buffet, or when we are in the middle of an exciting athletic competition or reading a good book or enjoying a dance, the thought will intrude. And when it does, it will cast a pall over the entire scene. The sounds of laughter will fade, for at least a while.

That's what life is like, that preacher reminded us. The stubborn fact of our mortality is always with us, and the knowledge of our eventual, certain death intrudes at the most inappropriate moments, bringing a shadow with it.

Although death is inevitable, we know somehow, in the depths of our hearts, that it is unnatural. Death doesn't make any sense to us. Why does this terror constantly stalk human existence? The Old Testament writer of the Book of Ecclesiastes, reflecting on the fragility and apparent meaninglessness of human existence, observes that God has "put a sense of past and future into their minds" (Ecclesiastes 3:11). Whatever life is about, we know that death should have no place in it.

However death might come — quickly, through accident, or slowly, through aging or disease — the prospect is not pleasant. For some, the terror of death is that it seems to render the whole of life ultimately meaninglessness. For others, it is the sadness at the prospect of separation from loved ones. For others still, it is the fear of what might lie on the other side. For most, death is fearsome because of all these things.

Cultures and civilizations in every place, in every age, have devised rituals and stories to help ease the transition through death. Often these have taken the form of attempting to appease powers on the other side who receive the spirit at death. Deep in the human heart lies the fear of possible terrors in the eternal sleep of death. What horrors might that final darkness hold?

Death is an enemy. It holds humanity captive. It laughs at our best efforts. We try not to think about it. We choose not to talk about it. Yet our culture is held tight in its icy grip — perhaps more than some other cultures because we deny it. We worship youth and beauty. We hide the signs of aging. Age is the enemy because the passing years bring us ever closer to the loss of strength and vigour, closer to our date with death.

In the New Testament, the Letter to the Hebrews addresses this fear, speaking of those who, because of their fear of death, live their whole lives in slavery. But the writer of this letter announces the end of death's power to enslave. The writer refers to the incarnation of Jesus (God entering the world as a person), to Jesus' death, and to his resurrection. The Good News is that the resurrection spells the ultimate defeat of death and the end of its power. Explaining what Jesus has done, the writer goes on to say:

> Since, therefore, the children [i.e., human beings] share flesh and blood, he himself [Jesus] likewise shared the same things, so that through death he might destroy the one who has the power of death, that is, the devil, and free those who all their lives were held in slavery by the fear of death (Hebrews 2:14–15).

Writing to an early community of Christian believers about the resurrection of Jesus and the fulfilment of God's purposes when the world comes to an end, St Paul writes:

> The saying that is written will be fulfilled:
> "Death has been swallowed up in victory."
> "Where, O death, is your victory?
> Where, O death, is your sting?"

"Thanks be to God," Paul exults, "who gives us the victory through our Lord Jesus Christ" (1 Corinthians 15:54, 55, 57). In the Gospel, we hear the Good News that Christ has won the decisive battle over death, and that the once formidable power of death is now only temporary. This is the ultimate good news in a culture that is traumatized by its fear and denial of death. In such a context, the work of evangelism is vital.

A Glimpse into the Heart of God

In the Parable of the Lost Son, told by Jesus in the fifteenth chapter of Luke's Gospel, we are given a glimpse into the heart of God as he surveys the human condition.

The story describes how a young and rather impetuous son took his share of his father's wealth and left home to go out on his own. Naïve, gullible, and foolish, he quickly spent his way through the money and ended up destitute. As he sat in squalor, contemplating his situation, he resolved to go home and ask his father if he could come back to work on the family farm as a hired hand. He started out for home, butterflies churning in his stomach, rehearing his speech as he walked, wondering if his father would even listen to him, perhaps dreading the speech his father might make.

The mortified young man had never been a father himself, so he had no possible way of knowing what was going on at home. He couldn't in his wildest dreams have imagined the scene that was being played out there day after day. The parents tossing sleeplessly in their beds, wondering about their son. Was he safe? Was he well? Was he happy? Was he managing to take care of himself? Were people somewhere taking advantage of him? Would they hear from him soon? Would they ever see him again? The son had no idea that as the father went about his work in the fields he was constantly looking up to scan the horizon in every direction, hoping for the appearance of that familiar figure coming down the road. Maybe today his boy would come home. The son knew nothing of this. He feared his father's anger; he dreaded his scorn and rejection.

Jesus says that while the boy was still a long way off, the father saw him. Of course he did! He had searched the horizon every day since his son had left, wondering, hoping, praying that this might be the day he would come home. The father ran to his son, he embraced him, he wept, he looked him over, he sent news to his neighbours, he organized a celebration. His son had come home! There was no speech, there was no scorn, no "I told you so's," no "I'll give you one last chance" — just pure joy, that the lost was found, that the one feared dead was alive.

In this parable, Jesus describes the heart of God aching for a lost world. The Gospel of Jesus Christ is a Gospel of reconciliation. God invites the lost and the hurting to come home, to be welcomed back into the family.

What's all the fuss about evangelism? It's about a broken world and a loving God. It's about a God who immerses himself in our situation in order to heal our pain and rescue us from evil. It's about a God who invites those who have heard and responded to this news to share it with others until the whole world knows.

CHAPTER TWO

What's the Good News?

More times now than I care to recall, I have heard the
sentiment expressed that everything we do in the Church
is evangelism. This statement betrays a serious misunderstanding of what evangelism is all about, and it needs to
be corrected if this important ministry is ever to regain its
right and proper place in the mission of the Church.

Not All Four-Legged Animals Are Dogs

Many years ago, as an undergraduate beginning to study
philosophy, I had a professor who liked to remind us that
not all four-legged animals are dogs. He was trying to teach
us the importance of reasoning in a logical manner, in
order to avoid invalid forms of argument and illegitimate
conclusions. "A dog is a four-legged animal," he would say,
holding up a picture of a dog. Then, holding up a picture
of a horse, he would continue, "This is a four-legged
animal; therefore, this must be a dog." He would point out
to us that there is something seriously wrong with any
form of argument that can logically conclude that a horse
must be a dog.

Sometimes, in church gatherings where evangelism is
being discussed, I think of that philosophy professor. The
participants in these discussions understand that evangelism is about sharing good news. They agree that the
people of God are a "good news people" and that good
news is for sharing. Unfortunately, at this point, the discussion frequently takes a wrong turn. What happens is
that someone remarks, "In this church we do lots of things

that are good news for people," and an animated conversation follows, in which the group members begin to list all the things they do that are experienced as good news by various groups of people.

Frequently, these activities are listed on newsprint and taped to the wall for everyone to look at and consider. An average church, in an exercise like this, can usually generate quite an impressive list within a few minutes. They point out that through their church the sick are visited in hospitals; the elderly are visited in nursing homes; the shut-ins are visited in their homes; the poor are given help with food, clothing, and shelter; the lonely are accepted into the church community; and the sad and grieving are given comfort and solace. They remind each other how they stand together in difficult times and how they support one another in times of need.

The next step in this process is obvious. If all these things we are doing are good news, the group reasons, then surely they must be evangelism. In fact, the participants conclude: "Everything we do is evangelism." But there is a serious error in logic here. Because evangelism means sharing good news, it does not necessarily follow that any and all good news is evangelism. I can almost hear the voice of my professor reminding us that not all four-legged animals are dogs. Misled by this faulty reasoning, the congregation is both pleased and amazed at how much they are already doing in the field of evangelism. They congratulate themselves and agree that they should keep up the good work. In the event that any new opportunities for good news activities should present themselves, everyone agrees that these should certainly be given serious consideration.

Now, obviously, churches should be involved in all the activities listed above, and many more. It is also important for church members to pause frequently, to remember and reflect upon the broad scope of activities carried out in their church. When church members have these types of conversations, they almost inevitably begin to feel better about their church and about themselves, and they are energized to keep up the good work. Such conversations and exercises are crucial to the health and vitality of congregational life.

My concern here is simply to point out that these good news activities, as important as they are, are not evangelism. They are certainly an important part of the mission of the Church as it seeks to serve the world in its brokenness and pain. It should go without saying that these ministries are also essential to the work of evangelism. When they are neglected and the Church appears to be unconcerned about the needs all around it, the ministry of evangelism will certainly lack integrity and effectiveness.

Nevertheless, evangelism is quite different from the important ministries of caring. It does not consist of just any good news or activity that helps people through difficult times or that makes them feel better about themselves. There is more to evangelism than doing nice things for people and showing that we truly care for them. The Good News that we are called to share through the ministry of evangelism has a specific content.

The Good News of the Gospel

In the New Testament, the Good News that God's people share in evangelism is described in two quite different ways. One uses the language of *reconciliation*; the other uses the language of God's *reign*. The former deals with God's eagerness to forgive sin and to welcome us into a new relationship of friendship and intimacy. The second has to do with the assurance that in the fullness of time, evil will be annihilated, and God's perfect will for creation and history will become the eternal reality.

These are not contradictory understandings of the Gospel, but two complementary strands that make up the complete message. They are like two sides of a coin. They must go together. We are reconciled with God in order to embrace and enter God's reign. We cannot embrace and enter God's reign (indeed, we would have no desire to do so) until we have experienced this reconciliation. When thinking about evangelism, there is frequently a temptation to embrace one of these strands to the virtual exclusion of the other. I have witnessed evangelistic discussions and presentations that have focused so exclusively on the theme of being reconciled to God that the theme of learning to live a new life under God's reign was barely mentioned. On the other hand, I have heard discussions of evangelism that focused so exclusively on declaring God's reign that the fact of human alienation from God (and the possibility of reconciliation) was completely overlooked. The one presentation sounds as though the Gospel is only about going to heaven when we die; the other sounds like a call to build the kingdom of God here on earth through our own efforts. On its own, without the balance of the other, each strand is a distortion.

The Good News Is about Reconciliation with God

In a passage summarizing the very essence of the Christian Gospel, St Paul writes:

> So if anyone is in Christ, there is a new creation: everything old has passed away; see, everything has become new! All of this is from God, who reconciled us to himself through Christ, and has given us the ministry of reconciliation; that is, in Christ God was reconciling the world to himself, not counting their trespasses against them, and entrusting the message of reconciliation to us. So we are ambassadors for

Christ, since God is making his appeal through us; we
entreat you on behalf of Christ, be reconciled to God. For
our sake he made him to be sin who knew no sin, so that
in him we might become the righteousness of God
(2 Corinthians 5:17–21).

It is difficult to miss the emphasis on reconciliation in this
passage. We know that talk of a need for reconciliation
indicates a relationship that has gone wrong. When we
encounter a passage like this, with such a pronounced
emphasis on reconciliation with God, we immediately
recognize the underlying assumption that our relationship
with God has gone wrong. This is the assumption that
drives the whole biblical story.

The Bible teaches that we have been created to live in
an intimate relationship with God, enjoying God's presence and sharing in God's purposes for creation and
history. It is within the context of this relationship (living
and working in partnership with God, enjoying God's
presence and friendship) that we experience wholeness
and fulfilment in our lives. But the Bible also teaches that
this relationship has sustained serious damage. The biblical story speaks of a terrible power that is at war with God,
seeking to frustrate God's purposes for history and to
destroy creation. In Scripture, this power is referred to in
different ways — as Evil, Death, Sin, Satan, or the Devil.
The seductive song of evil is that we have no need of God,
that we are quite capable of taking God's place as lord of
creation and history. With God out of the way, we would
be able to shape life the way we want it to be and experience the fullness of living totally independent lives. As it
is, we reason, God cramps our style by insisting that the
way of Christ is best.

The Bible indicates that human beings find this temptation to dismiss God from the picture to be irresistible. But
the promise that we will be better off without God turns

out to be a hideous lie, and the consequences of falling for it are beyond our ability to imagine. Seeking to dismiss God, humanity's "natural" state now becomes one of alienation from God, the one who gives us life and who gives life meaning. Within the biblical frame of reference, the pain and brokenness of this world, the injustices and abuses of power, the enormous complexity of our problems — all these result, at base, from our alienation from God and our collective determination to do things our way. Where God intended cosmic harmony, we now experience chaos and discord on every side.

Sometimes our alienation takes the form of active rebellion, in which we say an emphatic "no" to God, so we can say an equally emphatic "yes" to ourselves. Sometimes it takes the form of indifference, as God is simply ignored. Sometimes it takes the form of hostility, as God is blamed for all the evils and pain of this world. Frequently, I think, it takes the form of fear, as people suspect that God is against them rather than for them. I believe that much of what is expressed as hostility, indifference, or rebellion towards God is really, at a deeper level, a fear that somehow we need to find protection from God. That we need protection from God is one of evil's most sinister lies.

Fear of God

During the course of my years as a parish priest, I have come to believe that many people unintentionally look upon religion as a means of protecting themselves from God. For example, I have frequently found myself involved in earnest conversations with young parents who have contacted the church seeking baptism for their new baby. Very often these parents have had no active connection with any church for many, many years. They apparently come seeking baptism because they want to be good parents and somewhere in their background they acquired the idea that responsible parents have their children baptized. However, it has become clear to me in the course of these interviews that many of these young parents are really looking for some form of protection for their child against God.

When I ask them why they would like to have their child baptized, they frequently reply, "Just in case something happens." What they are saying is that if some unthinkable tragedy should occur and their baby should die, they want to make sure that God will accept their child into heaven. In their minds, they carry a picture or an idea of a God who will do terrible things to their precious child unless proper steps have been taken to prevent this. Their understanding is that in the mysterious, religious ritual of baptism, something happens that protects their child from God. As a priest, I am being asked if I will perform this ritual for them.

In the Gospel we hear the staggering truth that God is *for* us; *not against* us! We hear that even though we have wandered far away from God (believing these terrible lies, holding God at arm's length, perhaps deliberately ignoring or perhaps consciously rebelling against God, and openly doubting or feeling resentment), God is inviting us back. God is looking for reconciliation. God wants to be our friend. The message of the Gospel proclaims God's truth against the lies of evil and shines light into the darkness of the human situation. This truth is that, far from being out to get us, God wants to rescue us from evil. God wants to set us free from this horrible power, so we can live as we have always been intended to live.

God Wants to Be Your Friend

One summer evening, several years ago, my wife and I witnessed an event that I believe illustrates perfectly what the Christian Gospel is all about. It began after dinner when our six-year-old son asked if he could go to the corner store to buy some candy. Because he had to cross a very busy street, my wife and I went with him. We bought the candy and started for home. He rode ahead on his bike while we walked behind. We knew he wouldn't go too far ahead because he would have to wait for us at the next corner.

We walked along slowly, admiring lawns and gardens on the way. Then, as we approached the corner, we saw a marvellous sight. Benjamin was waiting there, straddling his bicycle, with his arms resting on the handlebars. Facing him was another boy of about the same age and size, similarly straddling his bicycle, with the same posture. The front wheels of their little bikes were touching each other, and the boys were leaning forward, each staring intently into the other's face. These boys had never seen each other before. As it turned out, the stranger and his family had moved into the neighbourhood only the day before — from a distant part of the country.

My wife and I stood back, watching the scene unfold before us. After a short silence, the new boy looked straight into Benjamin's face and said quietly, "Friends?" Benjamin looked back, nodded solemnly, and said "Friends." "Good!" the little fellow exclaimed, "I'll go and tell my mother if I can come to your house!" Not long afterwards, they were running around our lawn as if they had known each other all their lives. . . Benjamin and Travis became close friends. For two years, until both families moved, they were almost inseparable. They spent hours together, wading in the creek, climbing trees, building forts, throwing stones, telling stories, sharing secrets. They enjoyed each other's company and grew very close. What a wonderful friendship grew from that initial question, "Friends?" and the positive response, "Friends."

Over the years, I have spent a lot of time thinking about evangelism. I have thought about how the message of the Gospel can be presented in ways that people can clearly understand and how people can be helped to respond in appropriate ways. The more I think about it, the more I am convinced that in that innocent encounter between two young boys, I saw a remarkable picture of what evangelism is all about. As we go through life, busy with all the things that call upon our time, attention, and energy, God breaks into our consciousness and asks, quite simply, "Can we be friends?" God wants to be friends with us. This invitation to friendship with God is at the heart of the Gospel. In evangelism, this is the invitation we share.

The Good News Is about God's Reign

In the first chapter of Mark's Gospel, describing the beginnings of Jesus' ministry, we read: "Now after John was arrested, Jesus came to Galilee, proclaiming the good news of God, and saying, 'The time is fulfilled, and the kingdom of God has come near; repent, and believe in the good news'" (Mark 1:14–15). When Jesus came, the Good News he announced was about what he called the "kingdom of God." Jesus was not speaking of a specific geographical entity but rather of the fact of God's reign. As Jesus proclaimed this good news of God's reign, the people in Galilee could not possibly have guessed at the ultimate depths of what he was saying. Conditioned as they were by their own religious tradition, they probably thought he was promising them freedom from foreign occupation and the restoration of the past glories of their nation.

But Jesus was speaking of far more than the liberation of a tiny nation. He was proclaiming the liberation of all humanity from the power of evil; he was speaking of the eventual total destruction of evil and all that opposes God, in order that God's vision for creation and history might become the reality. God is still in control, Jesus was saying. Despite many appearances to the contrary, it is God's vision for history and creation that will ultimately prevail.

Evil has had a pretty good run. Its carnage and destruction are all around us. But when Jesus went into Galilee to begin his ministry, he served notice on evil. His ministry was the beginning of God's final offensive against its stranglehold. "The time is fulfilled," he said, "and the kingdom of God has come near" (Mark 1:15). With this announcement, he was declaring that there and then the offensive was being launched, that the battle for freedom was on, and that the outcome could not be in doubt.

Because God is for us, the news of God's reign is good news. God is not intervening in our situation in order to mess us up, but to clean up the mess that has already been made and to rescue us from evil and our own folly. The news of God's reign is the news of freedom, it is the promise that all will be put right. The news of God's reign is the news of wholeness and life. It is the news of eternal life, in a kingdom that knows nothing of sickness or tears or death.

The Good News Is about the Resurrection

What the people in Galilee and, later, Judea could not possibly have guessed was the role that Jesus would play in the coming of God's reign. Some thought that he was a prophet, bringing an important message to the nation from God. Some even dared to believe, in spite of all appearances, that this man with his little band of followers might become the king who would lead their nation to freedom. All these hopes were dashed at Calvary, where Jesus died a shameful death on the cross, and the people

gave voice to their disappointment with derision and
hostility.

But St Paul tells us that the foolishness of God is wiser
than human wisdom and the weakness of God is stronger
than human strength (1 Corinthians 1:25). The crucifixion
was Jesus' engagement with the powers of evil and death,
and his resurrection was proof that he had triumphed over
them. Death has always been the ultimate sign of evil's
control over creation. When Jesus rose from the dead,
notice was served that death had lost its power and that
its influence from now on would be limited. Its effects
would not be permanent, and in the fullness of God's
reign, there would be no death. In fact, death would be
entirely undone!

What exactly happened at Calvary is beyond our ability
to comprehend. Theologians and biblical scholars have
reflected upon it and debated about it for centuries —
indeed, for almost two millennia! It is enough for us to
understand that there are two main strands of interpretation that run through the New Testament. These two
strands correspond to the two strands of reconciliation
and God's reign that make up the Gospel message.

The *reconciliation* strand emphasizes the fact that
Christ's death and resurrection are a *sacrifice* that allows
us to be forgiven for everything that has separated us from
God. This then brings us into a new relationship with God.
When we were under the power of evil, believing its lies,
we did many things in opposition to God. Sometimes we
acted consciously and intentionally; at other times, we had
no idea we were working against God's purposes. Often
we simply ignored God and lived entirely for ourselves and
our own desires. God wasn't even on the farthest horizon
of our thoughts.

This lack of concern for, or even opposition to, God's
purposes for history and creation are what the Bible
describes as sin. Sinful actions are those that run contrary

to God's purposes for the world, for the people of God, and for the future. In speaking of sin, it is important for us to understand that the Bible does not say that we are sinners because we commit sins. It is the other way round. We commit sins because we are sinners. It is inevitable that we will go against God. To be a sinner means that our imaginations and our wills have been affected so deeply that we tragically think we are better off by choosing not to live under God's grace, to honour God's purposes, or even to bother finding out what those purposes might be. We simply decide that we will let something else drive our actions and our desires. Most frequently, but not always, that something else is self-interest.

The individual actions and attitudes that are *labelled* as sins are symptoms of the fact that our imaginations and wills have been radically damaged by the power of evil. The biblical story tells us that we have all been affected in this way; we all fall short of God's intentions for us, whether from open rebellion or passive neglect. Set against the backdrop of the Old Testament language and imagery of sacrifice, the New Testament writers explain that Jesus gave himself as the perfect and complete sacrifice for our sins, so that forgiveness might be possible for us. Because of Jesus' death and resurrection, we can be forgiven and start all over again with God.

The *reign* strand of the Gospel puts emphasis on the fact that, because of Christ's death and resurrection, evil has lost its power to hold us captive any longer! Jesus has come like a freedom fighter, gone behind the enemy lines, and set us free! We were helpless prisoners of war. Our hearts, our minds, and our imaginations had been taken captive by evil. We feared, resented, ignored, and dismissed God. But now we have been liberated. Now we can welcome God's presence into our lives and begin to live for God's purposes. We can willingly choose to turn from our present allegiances in order to embrace and enter

God's reign. We can consider ourselves dead to the power of sin but alive to the presence and purposes of God. We can become totally new people, being changed by God's power into the people we were created to be.

Death has always been the ultimate sign of evil's power in this world. Through his resurrection, Jesus has shown that death's power is now only temporary. Death will never be the last word in God's creation. Because evil's defeat is now certain, we can trust that the final word for history and creation will belong to God. It is God's will that will be done.

The two strands of reconciliation and reign are intertwined through the New Testament. What they come down to is this: Loving us deeply and sensing our plight, God reached out to us in Jesus. Jesus fought the battle with evil that we couldn't fight for ourselves and made it possible for us to be set free. As captives of evil, with flawed and damaged wills, we have often acted in opposition, even in hostility, to God. But God offers us forgiveness and invites us to come back. God offers us the deepest, most exciting, most accepting, and yet most challenging friendship we will ever have.

In the New Testament letter to the church in Rome, St Paul writes these words:

> While we were still weak, at the right time Christ died for the ungodly. Indeed, rarely will anyone die for a righteous person — though perhaps for a good person someone might actually dare to die. But God proves his love for us in that while we still were sinners Christ died for us (Romans 5:6–8).

The good news that we share in evangelism is the news of God's love, and the fact that God has not abandoned us. It is the news that even now God's reign is breaking in and that, in the fullness of time, God's perfect reign will be fully realized. It is the news about the possibility of reconciliation with God, forgiveness of sins, freedom from evil, a new life lived in harmony with the purposes of God, and freedom from the tyranny and fear of death. In such a world as ours, this is good news indeed. As followers of Jesus and members of his Church, this is the good news we are commissioned to share.

CHAPTER THREE

You're Invited: R.S.V.P.

My wife and I recently received the news that a long-time friend is about to be married. This news came in the form of an invitation which did three things: it announced that the wedding was going to take place, giving the details of time and location; it invited us to attend; and it asked us to reply so they would know whether or not we were coming to the celebration. Since we were very pleased to hear about the wedding and to be invited as guests, we replied immediately, saying that we would love to attend.

I am glad we received notice of the wedding through an invitation rather than a news release. If I had learned of the couple's wedding plans through an announcement in the local paper, I would have been happy for them but I wouldn't really have felt included. Although the announcement might have contained exactly the same good news as the invitation, I much preferred the invitation, because it included me in the celebration.

In thinking about evangelism, it is important to remember that the Good News of the Gospel is never simply an announcement. The Gospel's most natural form is an invitation. When Jesus came into Galilee "proclaiming the Good News of God," he was doing more than simply passing on information. He was issuing an invitation. He wanted his hearers to know that they were included in the Good News, and he wanted them to respond. So he concluded his announcement with the invitation to "repent and believe the good news" (Mark 1:15).

Although the word "repent" might cause some of us to conjure up images of hair shirts and ashes, Jesus was actually inviting the people to turn from their lesser pre-occupations and to experience the richness and freedom of God's reign. He was asking them to recognize and choose God's reign from all the options available to them, to enter it freely and voluntarily, and to bring their lives into line with this new reality. Similarly, when St Paul spoke of the possibility of reconciliation with God through Christ, he was not simply making an announcement. He wanted those who heard the news to realize that they were included in God's gracious offer and to accept it. He shared the news in the form of an invitation and asked for a response. "We entreat you on behalf of Christ," he wrote, "be reconciled to God" (2 Corinthians 5:20). The natural form of the Gospel is invitation. It is news, certainly; good news, to be sure. But more than anything, it is invitation. It never merely informs; it always invites.

Invitations Expect a Response

The thing about an invitation is that its sender expects a response. When we are invited to a wedding or a party, we have to decide whether or not to accept the invitation. When someone asks whether we would like to be friends with them, or when someone proposes marriage to us, they are expecting an answer. At some point, failure to make a definite decision means that we have actually decided not to accept the invitation. When the Gospel is shared, it anticipates a response. When we receive an invitation, we usually know what constitutes an appropriate response. In order to be effective in evangelism, we must know what constitutes an appropriate response to the invitation of the Gospel.

At the most basic level, the response that the Gospel seeks is a simple "yes." Spoken in reply to the invitation to be reconciled with God through Jesus Christ, and to enter the reign of God, the simple word "yes" becomes the most profound prayer in all the world. With this prayer, we indicate our willingness to accept God's offer of reconciliation and our readiness to begin learning a whole new way of life that will bring us the deepest possible satisfaction, because it is in harmony with God's purposes.

The simplicity of this response can be deceptive, however, because the intention and commitment it represents will eventually permeate every area of our lives and have a profound effect upon the way we think, act, and choose. Many years ago, I asked a young woman if she would marry me. After a few seconds of silence, which seemed like an eternity to me, she very quietly said, "Yes." With that one word, and the commitment it represented, a whole new future unfolded that affected every area of our lives. So it is with God's invitation in the Gospel. It marks the beginning of an entirely new future. With this "yes," we begin the adventure of learning to live a new way of life, with different goals and different priorities. This is a commitment that sets the direction for the rest of our lives.

It is worth noting here that different traditions use different phrases to describe what happens when one hears this invitation, accepts it, and begins this new life. Some speak of "becoming a Christian," some of "accepting Christ"; others speak of "being saved" or of "being born again." In the Anglican Church in Canada I have often heard clergy speak of "growing into one's baptism." Each of these phrases points to the same reality. Personally, I prefer the phrase "becoming a follower of Jesus," because it is sufficiently open ended to avoid a narrow exclusivity, while capturing so clearly the essence of what this new life is all about.

Life in Three Dimensions

The new life that we begin to live when we say "yes" to God does not come naturally to us. We have to learn how to live it. We have to grow into it. It is helpful to think of this new life as having three dimensions, which, though quite distinct from each other, are tightly interwoven. These dimensions are the personal, the corporate, and the public. In saying "yes" to God, we are committing ourselves to learning and growing in each of these areas.

1. The Personal Dimension: Becoming a "Child of God"

In saying "yes" to the invitation of the Gospel, I am saying "yes" to becoming a child of God. In the first chapter of John's Gospel we read these words about those who received the message of Jesus: "to all who received him, who believed in his name, he gave power to become children of God, who were born, not of blood or of the will of the flesh or of the will of man, but of God" (John 1:12–13). This dimension of the new life is intensely intimate and individual. It has to do with my personal and individual response to God and our ongoing relationship. In this area I am concerned with nurturing and deepening my walk with God. I work to develop the spiritual disciplines of Scripture reading and prayer, because I want to grow in my understanding of God's character and ways. I want to become more and more aware of God's presence in my life and to be alive to the signs of God's activity around me. I want to be able to trace God's footprints along the pathways of my life and to hear the echo of God's voice calling to me through the course of my daily activities.

To this dimension belong questions of identity and character, of personal ethics and behaviour. It is here that I accept God's forgiveness for the waywardness and sinfulness of my own life and take on my new identity as a child of God. I commit myself to learning to live in ways that are pleasing to God, and I open myself to the process of transformation by which God's Spirit will work in me to make me more and more the person I am meant to become. The goal of this process is to become more and more like Jesus and to understand ever more deeply what it means to follow him. And the more I become like Jesus, the more I become myself.

As this relationship develops and deepens, I find that my goals and aspirations for the future come into conflict with God less and less. They are coloured, more and more, by my understanding of what God is calling me to do. I develop a growing understanding that I am being called to participate in the work of reconciling the whole world to God, and I discover that God has equipped me to take my place in this work. I come to see that it is this friendship with God, and my sharing in the work of reconciliation, that gives my life its meaning and its direction. More and more this new relationship shapes the way I think about myself and influences how I live. It colours the choices that I make, the criteria by which I evaluate my life, and the way I structure my priorities. I come to see myself as a steward (a servant) offering God my time, talent, and resources in the service of the work of reconciliation.

Authentic evangelism recognizes this *personal* dimension of the Gospel invitation. It includes the invitation for people to turn, personally and individually, to Christ, in order to be reconciled to God, to enter God's reign, and to begin learning how to live their personal lives in the light of this new reality.

2. The Corporate Dimension:
The People of God

The individual dimension of our response is important, but it is not the whole story. When we say "yes" to the Gospel invitation, we are also saying yes to becoming a part of the people of God. Sometimes, in our highly individualistic society, this aspect of Christian faith is downplayed or neglected altogether. To the degree that this is so, the version of the Gospel being presented is an aberration of authentic Christian faith.

It is essential to a proper understanding of the Gospel to realize that God's purposes in this world go far beyond rescuing isolated individuals from their plight and initiating private and personal relationships with each of them independently of one another. Far beyond reconciling isolated individuals, God wants to reconcile people to one another as well. The Christian community is both a result and a sign of this reconciling work of God. From beginning to end, the Christian faith is a *corporate* faith, and the biblical story is the story of a people. As we read the biblical story, it is clear that God chooses to work in this world through a special community of people, whom he calls out and sets aside. In its beginning, this community was as small as the immediate family of Abraham; in time, it grew to embrace the entire nation of Israel. In the New Testament it consists of the Church — that is, the company of those who have embraced the Gospel and turned to become followers of Jesus.

The Gospel invitation, while addressed to individuals, is an invitation to join this community. It is impossible to accept the individual invitation without becoming part of the community; the two aspects of the new life are inseparable. The only honest response to the comment "I can be a good Christian without being a part of the Church" is "That is an impossibility." The very thought is a heresy, a misunderstanding born of an age of highly prized individualism that is entirely foreign to biblical ways of thinking.

The Church is a community of people with a very special identity and calling. We are the community that has heard and accepted the Gospel invitation of reconciliation with God through Jesus Christ. Beyond enjoying this state of reconciliation and renewed relationship with God for our own sakes, we are now commissioned to work for the reconciliation of the whole world to God. Our life together in the local church is to be a model of what this reconciliation looks like, and a sign of the efficacy of Christ's work as we learn to love one another truly and to live as God intends us to live.

Being reconciled with God implies being reconciled with each other. Jesus made it very clear that those who accept God's forgiveness must be prepared to forgive one another and to live at peace with each other. The New Testament letters to the various churches are filled with instructions regarding the common life of these fledgling communities. The goal of all these instructions is to shape the community in such a way that it models God's reconciliation. The virtues on which these instructions are based are those that create and nurture community; the corrosive and explosive sins that they warn against are those that destroy community.

In its common life this community is concerned with such things as public worship, the communal reading of Scripture, corporate prayer, the public proclamation of the Gospel, and the celebration of the Sacraments. Through these, the community is not only nurtured; it also witnesses to the presence and work of God in the world. The members learn that, far from being independent individuals, they belong to one another like the different parts of a body. Each person is gifted in such a way as to be able to contribute uniquely and significantly to the overall health and well-being of the community. The members love one another, care for one another, and encourage and support one another. They model the interdependence and mutual care that God desires for creation, which have been so terribly distorted by sin. In a way, the community is called to function as a working model of the world the way God would like it to be. This community, as it learns to live out its calling as the people of God, is a preview in miniature of the world God is preparing for the future.

This is not to say that the Church's members are perfect! They are not; they are ordinary people, weak and sinful, who are learning to live, sometimes with difficulty, under God's grace. What makes this community stand out is the love that its members are learning to share with one another, as they learn to overlook faults and imperfections, to be patient and caring with one another, to put the best possible interpretation on every situation, and to encourage one another to continue to grow in faith and in love. In a world that works from the premise of self-interest, the formation of such authentic community is as great a miracle of grace as the salvation of individual souls. The ability of the Gospel to form such communities out of ordinary, self-willed people is the test of its authenticity. The community of the Church is proof to the powers of darkness that they have been defeated by Christ, and that their days are numbered.

Evangelism, when it is done well, will clearly present the invitation to join in the life of the people of God.

3. The Public Dimension: The Reign of God

In many parts of our society today there is an assumption that religious belief and commitment are private matters that have no place in the public arena. This attitude is frequently found in the Church as well. Disgruntled church members wonder why their leaders are making statements about public issues that really do not seem to have anything to do with the sphere of religion, or they stare in bewilderment as they are asked to make an attempt to share their faith with someone with no apparent faith connections. What does this have to do with being Christian, they wonder? Surely my personal beliefs are a private matter between God and me. Why is the Church so interested in going public?

Just as surely as the Gospel invitation has both a *personal* and a *community, or corporate*, dimension, so it has a *public* dimension. We have said that God's purposes do not end with the individual. Nor do they end with the Church. The biblical vision is that God's reign will cover the whole earth. Those who have been reconciled with God are learning to say "yes" to this vision. The children of God, individually, and the people of God, collectively, are learning to look beyond themselves to God's vision for the world. Ultimately, our mission is to work for the reconciliation of the whole world to God. This includes the whole of humankind, the entire created order, and all the institutions and structures of this world.

We, as the Church, are called to *serve* in the public sphere. In the name of Jesus, we are called to serve this world in its brokenness, addressing its hurts, its injustices, its bewilderment, and its oppression. We seek to reach out in compassion to victims of human oppression and the ravages of a natural world gone awry from the effects of sin. We are also meant to *proclaim* the way of Christ when confronted with issues of public justice and liberation. We are concerned to take up the cause of the oppressed and to speak for those who have no voice. We address social sins like racism, sexism, poverty, and exploitation. Inspired by the biblical vision of a world living freely, under the just and perfect reign of God, we address social ills in order to relieve the plight of the broken and oppressed. We seek to become the human instruments of God's mercy and compassion. In addition to ministries of compassion and mercy, we are called to engage the power structures of this world with the vision of God's justice, and to all, victim and oppressor alike, we are called to declare the Lordship of Christ and the reign of God.

But as surely as we have been called to minister to the world in its brokenness, so have we been called to work for the conversion of the world. We have been charged with the responsibility of *inviting* people to accept the Good News that, through Jesus Christ, reconciliation with God is possible. We have been entrusted with the privilege of inviting people everywhere to be reconciled with God. The sharing of this Good News and the invitation to reconciliation constitute the evangelizing component of our mission. To the degree that we fail to do this, we are being unfaithful to our calling.

As we grow in our understanding of this public dimension of the Gospel, we come to see quite clearly that the decision to become a follower of Jesus really does affect every area of life. We seek to bring our whole life in line with the vision of God's reign, allowing it to inform our values, the practices we champion, and the decisions and choices we make. We realize that in all that we do, and wherever we go, we are ambassadors of God's reign.

A Balanced Response

One important thing to keep in mind is that a balanced response to the Gospel invitation requires that the individual eventually embrace all three dimensions of the new life: the personal, the corporate, and the public. Human nature being what it is, most of us, for various reasons, will naturally feel more attracted to one or two of these dimensions, and less attracted to the other one or two. The danger is that we might be tempted to regard the dimension with which we feel most familiar and comfortable as "true" Christianity and to look down on the other two dimensions as being somehow inferior. At the very least, those who feel most at home in one or other of these dimensions often look with suspicion upon those who feel most comfortable in a different dimension.

A person who naturally enjoys the corporate dimension, for example, might tend to dismiss the people in the individual dimension as overly enthusiastic and subjective, and those in the public dimension as mere "do-gooders." One who feels most comfortable in the public dimension might dismiss those in the individual dimension as being too preoccupied with their own spirituality, and those in the corporate dimension as interested only in maintaining an institution. One who feels most comfortable in the individual dimension might dismiss those in the corporate dimension as merely "nominal" Christians, and those in the public dimension as "Social Gospellers," who are perhaps not Christian at all.

There may be some truth in a few of these statements, but that is hardly the point. What is important is not to argue about which of these dimensions represents "authentic" Christian faith, but rather to see that every growing Christian must eventually embrace all three dimensions as part of his or her Christian lifestyle. All Christians need to recognize the importance of all three dimensions in a balanced and fruitful Christian life.

Those whose primary experience of Christian faith is in the *individual* dimension must come to see the importance of the Church in the purposes of God. They cannot simply dismiss the Body of Christ as irrelevant to their "personal walk with God"; they must instead become active participants in the life of the Church, learning what it means to live as members of the Body of Christ and taking their place in its ministry and support. Likewise, they must move into the public dimension, learning what it means to confess that Christ is Lord in every area of life. They must develop a Christian mind that allows them to discern God's presence in all areas of life and to understand God's purposes for the whole of creation.

Those whose formative experience of Christian faith is in the *corporate* dimension must come to see that God invites them into a highly personal relationship. They must understand that God knows them individually and calls them by name. They cannot use the Christian community as a place in which to hide from God; they must come before him personally and embrace Christ for themselves, opening themselves as individuals to developing a friendship with God and to the process of personal transformation through God's Spirit. Likewise, they must come to embrace the mission of the Church in the world. They cannot be content with the mere survival of the Church community. The Church exists for mission in the public arena and they must eventually take their place in that mission.

Those whose Christian experience is primarily in the *public* dimension must likewise take care to develop deep roots in the Christian community for worship and nurture, and to develop the personal disciplines that lead to spiritual growth. Failure to move into the individual and corporate dimensions of Christian experience may well eventually undermine what is being fought for in the public dimension.

Three Doors for Evangelism

Because of the rich diversity in human personality and experience, I believe that each of these dimensions of Christian living presents an opportunity for evangelism. Each of them offers a door through which people can be led to follow Jesus.

There are many who sense a spiritual vacuum in their lives. They yearn for a sense of connection with God. Others are aware of their need to be forgiven, while others are simply tired of their weakness and are longing for some power that will help them to somehow become better people. For these, and many more, the invitation to become a child of God, to be reconciled to God, and to develop a personal friendship with God, will be eagerly heard. They can be led through the door of the *individual* dimension.

Many people in our society are lonely. Others suffer from various forms of brokenness or carry deep hurts and anguish. Still others are searching for hope, wondering whether life has any meaning at all. For these and many others, the invitation to join a loving, accepting, worshipping, celebrating, teaching, nurturing community will be like refreshing rain on parched ground. They are ready to enter through the door of the *corporate* dimension.

There are many good people in this world who long to see justice prevail and who work long and hard to relieve the plight of the suffering and the oppressed, or to save the environment from further pollution and destruction. Many of these tireless, selfless workers have long since given up on the Church and on Christianity, having judged it to be completely unconcerned about and irrelevant to the causes that so passionately motivate them. But, in truth, they are very close to the heart of God. They are, in fact, actively engaged in the very activities that bring joy to the heart of God. When the Church is actively engaged in the public arena, Christians will encounter many of these dedicated workers, with no apparent commitment to Christ or the Church. If Christians help them see that their hearts beat close to the heart of God, perhaps they can be led through the door of the *public* dimension, to eventually become enthusiastic and committed followers of Jesus.

Once a person has entered through the appropriate door, continued instruction and nurture in the faith will allow him or her to participate, in good time, in the other dimensions as well. The important point here is to recognize that each of these three dimensions represents an open door for evangelism.

The Authentically Evangelized Person

All of this leads us to the question of what an authentically evangelized person looks like. In other words, what has changed for the person who has heard the Gospel invitation and said, "Yes"? The shortest answer to this question is the single word *everything*. As St Paul puts it in his Second Letter to the Corinthians, "If anyone is in Christ, there is a new creation; everything old has passed away; see, everything has become new!" (2 Corinthians 5:17). To the person who has recognized the dawning of God's reign in Christ and who has chosen to take part in it, a whole new world appears. This person begins to learn to live a new life. It is just like being "born again."

The person who says "yes" to Christ and turns to follow him, becomes, in effect, a new person, with a new perspective, a new purpose, and a new power. The new perspective is that of God's reign. A whole new set of values now comes into play, an entirely different way of looking at life from the perspective of God's purposes for creation and history. The newly committed follower of Jesus discovers that life has a new purpose. Whatever he or she lived for previously, the objective now is to live a life that is pleasing to Christ. The creed of the Christian is "Jesus is Lord." There is nothing simple about this. It would take more than a lifetime to learn this new life perfectly, and progress often seems painfully slow, but at least the direction is clear. Again, to quote St Paul from Second Corinthians, as Christians, "those who live might live no longer for themselves, but for him who died and was raised for them" (2 Corinthians 5:15).

Fortunately, God does not leave us to work all this out on our own, in our own strength. The promise of Scripture is that God makes the power of his Holy Spirit available to all who turn to Christ, in order to enable us to live this new life. (The eighth chapter of the Letter to the Romans describes in some detail the work of the Holy Spirit in the life of those who turn to Christ.)

Certainty, by the Grace of God

The invitation to turn to Christ, and the new life that he offers, are freely given gifts that can never be earned. The Gospel invitation is not extended on the basis of merit, but as the free gift of God, based on the destruction of death through Christ's crucifixion and resurrection. St Paul explained it this way in writing to the Christians in the city of Ephesus: "For by grace you have been saved through faith, and this is not your own doing; it is the gift of God — not the result of works, so that no one may boast" (Ephesians 2:8–9). When I was a small boy, a Sunday school teacher taught me the meaning of the word *grace* with this acronym: **G**reat **R**iches **A**t **C**hrist's **E**xpense.

We do not earn a chance at reconciliation with God; we do not earn our way into God's kingdom. These are offered freely, to all who will accept. For those who accept, a whole new life opens up. The adventure of learning to live this new life begins with the simple word *yes*.

One of the reasons, I think, that many people in our churches find it difficult to think about engaging in evangelism is that they are not certain whether they themselves are "authentic" Christians. They hope they are, but they are never quite sure. Recently, in a class I was teaching on Christian basics, I asked the participants what questions they hoped to have answered during the course. One person, a good churchgoer for many years, said, "I want to find out how I can know that I am really in." After all these years in the Church, this person was still not quite sure of being a Christian. Quite apart from its negative impact on evangelism, I think that this is a tragedy.

Because our acceptance by God is based on grace rather than merit, there is no need to worry or wonder about whether or not we are included. The invitation is offered to all of us; our part is simply to respond. We can move from being seekers (or perhaps hopers, with our fingers crossed) to being followers, simply by acknowledging the invitation and saying, "Yes." This is a short word, but in terms of the Gospel invitation, it is the pivotal point between two very different worlds. After "yes," we begin learning how to live a whole new life.

The ministry of evangelism is for those who have said a clear and heartfelt "yes." The goal of evangelism is to help others to understand the nature and implications of this invitation and to say "yes" for themselves.

CHAPTER FOUR

Understanding Reluctance

Most people welcome the opportunity to share good news with others. My younger children frequently argue about who will have the privilege of telling me something they think is important. But this is not true of evangelism. The mere mention of the word is usually enough to make most of us feel uncomfortable at best and threatened at worst. So we have to address the question: "If evangelism is sharing good news, why does the *call* to evangelism so frequently feel like *bad news?*"

Suspicions and Stereotypes

Charlatans

I believe that much of the hesitancy around evangelism can be attributed to negative stereotypes associated with the word. Some of us have seen too many slick, high-powered "preachers" on television, and we know that these creatures describe themselves as evangelists. We have watched them, with their expensive suits and jewellery and every hair sprayed perfectly into place, as they waved their Bibles around and emotionally manipulated the gullible and needy. We have been disgusted by their shameless appeals for money and have felt further repulsed as scandals concerning financial and sexual indiscretions have come to light. If the call to evangelism has anything to do with this, we think to ourselves, how could anyone with common sense and integrity even consider having anything to do with it?

Unwelcome Intrusions

Some of us have been bothered at our doors, feeling our privacy invaded by uninvited and confrontational visitors. They didn't seem to get the hint when we tried to suggest that we weren't really interested. They persisted in asking us personal questions, making us feel inadequate and uneasy. We didn't want to be rude to them, but we didn't want this encounter either. We felt tense, and we resented their calling. If evangelism means that I will be asked to go knocking on doors, we think to ourselves, bothering and embarrassing people in their homes or possibly standing on streetcorners handing out Christian literature, I don't want any part of it. When we hear the word mentioned, chances are that we simply tune out.

"Religious Fanatics"

Some of us have had a relative or a co-worker whom we could fairly describe as a "religious fanatic." They most likely had an amazing (and annoying) genius for turning every possible topic of conversation into a discussion about religion. They were probably also quite certain that they possessed the whole truth and that the rest of us were simply wrong. They either tried to make us feel guilty or badgered us so much to become like them that we began to wish we could avoid any further contact with them. If evangelism is about becoming an insensitive, single-minded, religious fanatic, we think to ourselves, count me out.

So much of what seems to be associated with popular, contemporary evangelism appears to be manipulative and insensitive. The needs of the so-called evangelists seem to be primary; the needs of their audience secondary. We feel as though Jesus himself would find their methods, and probably their motives, distasteful. In the light of these stereotypes, who could blame us for being wary? Evangelism has developed a bad reputation.

Suspicions of Self-Interest and Empire Building

For others, the problem with the renewed emphasis on evangelism in the Church is an uneasy sense that it might be self-serving. We know only too well that many churches are going through difficult times. Attendance is down, financial contributions are down, congregations are aging, there is less money, and there are fewer hands to do all that has to be done. Is this sudden interest in evangelism, they wonder, really just a way of pumping up the numbers on the members' list?

I read recently a comment from a disgruntled former pastor whose congregation had replaced him because they thought he had not shown enough leadership in evangelism. "For them," he said ruefully, "evangelism was really a Greek word for body count." In a similar vein, I once heard a church consultant remark that as he visited a number of churches, helping them with matters relating to congregational vitality, he had unwittingly discovered a new model of "church growth" in operation. He called it the "vampire model." Its slogan could have been "We need some new blood around here." Such people were not talking about how the ministries of their church could help people in need, but about how they could find more people to help the church in *its* time of need. The uneasiness with this sense that evangelism has to do with recruitment comes from an underlying conviction that the church should not be trying to recruit people simply for survival.

Some also fear that evangelism has something to do with empire building. Perhaps they feel that the clergy or church leadership have been taken in by the "bigger is better" mentality, or that there is some pride on the line here, a desire to see how big a church they can build. Somehow they sense that their church should not be preoccupied with numbers. It should not be out hunting for scalps just to create an appearance of success.

A negative response to these suspicions and stereotypes is perfectly understandable, but we cannot use them as an excuse for dismissing evangelism out of hand. Committed Christians face the challenge of doing everything in our power to rescue this important ministry from the charlatans who abuse it and the keen but clueless who misuse it, and to develop sensitive ways of evangelizing that are true to the Gospel, honouring to Christ, and in harmony with our own temperament and ethos.

Societal Issues

Pluralism, Tolerance, and Relativism
Societal issues also contribute to a feeling of uncertainty about evangelism. Perhaps the most important of these is our societal commitment, as Canadians, to pluralism. In our society, we rightly place a high value on pluralism and tolerance. We willingly embrace a diversity of lifestyles, worldviews, and belief systems, giving one another the right to live in accordance with our varying traditions, beliefs, and convictions. At the same time, we try to accept one another and to live together in harmony. It should not be surprising that since we have been conditioned by our culture to think spontaneously in terms of pluralism and tolerance, we should have a certain hesitancy about evangelism. Who are we, we ask ourselves, to be interfering with someone else's choices or beliefs? What right do we have to attempt to persuade them to take our point of view?

The problem here is that pluralism easily shades into relativism. But there are important differences between pluralism and relativism. Pluralism allows for recognition of a diversity of lifestyles and belief systems and for the right of people to choose their own path. Relativism goes beyond this, to affirm that all belief systems are equally true, and it doesn't really matter which system one eventually chooses. Pluralism says that we have the right to choose, and that our choice should be honoured and respected. Relativism says that ultimately it makes little difference what choice we make. All the options are equally true; all the choices are equally valid. Truth is eventually determined on the basis of whatever "works best" for any given person. If Christianity works for you, that's fine; if shopping works for me, that's fine too.

Christians can and should embrace pluralism with enthusiasm, but should deny relativism with equal passion. With pluralism, we recognize that there is a whole marketplace of ideas, philosophies, and worldviews out there competing for our allegiance; as Christians we should be standing up in this marketplace, making the case for Christianity in as compelling a way as we can. On the other hand, relativism cuts the heart out of vital Christian faith.

Christianity centres on the conviction that at a particular time in history, in a particular life, God acted in a particular way. God has been revealed to us uniquely in Jesus of Nazareth and God has acted decisively in his life, death, and resurrection to launch the only effective offensive against the powers of darkness to set creation free. When Christianity surrenders this conviction about the uniqueness of Jesus Christ, in terms of who he is and what he has done, it surrenders its very core.

To be effective in the ministry of evangelism, we must learn to distinguish between pluralism and relativism. We cannot surrender the conviction that, in Jesus, God has entered our world, that Jesus is the only way to reconciliation with God and to the new life that God offers. Following the example of the first apostles, our call is to go into the marketplace of ideas, proclaiming the good news about Jesus and the resurrection, attempting to persuade as many as we can to acknowledge that Jesus is Lord and to turn to him. Vital Christian faith results in a passionate response to this call.

It should go without saying that this work of evangelism is to be done in a spirit of gentleness and genuine humility. There is no place in this ministry for feelings of arrogance, superiority, or imperialism. Those who wish to receive a hearing will seek to make their case clearly, combining conviction with compassion. Certainly, we must give others permission to believe as they wish. After all, if God is willing to do so, how could we do less? But God also wants everyone to hear the good news about Jesus and to be given the opportunity to respond. This is the challenge facing the people of God in a pluralistic society.

Cynicism

Another societal issue that tends to reinforce hesitancy concerning evangelism is an apparently widespread cynicism about authority in general and organized religion in particular. People are jaded and wary. Every day they are bombarded by thousands of sales pitches. They are suspicious of their politicians, merchants, and neighbours. People have put up their defences and become cynical. They are simply not willing to accept at face value anything they are told.

This cynicism transfers quite naturally to the world of organized religion. Many people are not willing to grant that Christian preachers might be telling the truth. They assume that there is a hidden agenda, that somehow the preacher has an angle that will prove to be more self-serving than self-giving. Many suspect that the main agenda of the Church is to relieve them of as much of their money as it can. Unfortunately, this cynicism is reinforced by the fact that many people have simply decided that, whether or not it has the truth, by and large the Church is irrelevant to their lives and concerns. Dull services, boring sermons, pitches for money — these are the things many people almost instinctively think about when they hear the word *church*.

Still others are nursing grievances against the Church, some of which are well deserved. It wasn't so long ago that the Church had more power in the lives of people than it does today, and that power was often exercised in negative ways. For many people, the Church was not a community of healing and good news; all it did was make them feel guilty and unworthy. As a parish priest, I regularly hear stories of lament, complaint, and often deep anger when people talk of their previous experiences with church life. If they are telling these stories to me, you can be sure they are also telling them to their friends and neighbours. This does little for the reputation of the Church as a place of good news.

Combine this with what is more often than not a negative portrayal of the Church in movies, on TV, and in the press — and it is easy to understand the cynicism with which many people regard the Church. And in such a cultural climate, it is frightening to witness to the Gospel. It is far easier to remain undercover.

There is one bright light in this rather bleak picture: disillusionment with the Church does not automatically translate into disillusionment with Christian faith or, to be more precise, with Jesus himself. My personal experience is that there are many people who are openly interested in Jesus and who welcome the opportunity to talk about him and learn about him. The counterpoint to the cynicism of the age is a wide open spiritual hunger, as people look for wholeness and meaning.

The Condition of the Church

For some people, hesitation about evangelism has to do with the condition of their church. I have frequently heard people remark that they would, quite frankly, be embarrassed to invite their friends to come to church with them because of what happens there. The line of reasoning is that they are happy to attend themselves because their friends are there and they feel quite comfortable. Unfortunately, they are aware that their non-Christian friends would look at the situation through different eyes and have a very different experience.

They fear that these friends would find the service lifeless, the music outdated, the preaching irrelevant, the buildings in need of maintenance, and possibly, the congregation cold and aloof. There is a mutual frustration between clergy and laity here. I have heard laypeople comment that they don't invite their friends to church because of the preaching; I have heard clergy express their frustration that people in their congregations are not friendly towards visitors and newcomers, preferring to spend coffee hour after the service with their friends. Believe it or not, I have even heard clergy admit that they wouldn't attend their own churches if they weren't being paid to do so! Sooner or later, evangelism leads to an invitation to attend church. If we can't invite friends to come with us to church without apologizing or feeling embarrassed about what they might find there, it doesn't do much to bolster our enthusiasm for evangelism.

Lack of Confidence

All these explanations for hesitancy about evangelism are, I believe, valid. But I do not think they are the main reasons. In fact, sometimes I suspect that they are used as excuses to avoid the true causes — which, I believe, have to do with a lack of confidence.

Lack of Confidence in Ourselves

Our lack of confidence in ourselves to do the work of evangelism is sometimes related to the way evangelism is presented and the models that we are given. Efforts to inspire people about evangelism are frequently quite insensitive, resulting in feelings of guilt and discomfort more than in positive action. Nothing discourages the average church member more than hearing about the exploits of some highly extroverted, charismatic, persuasive, naturally gifted evangelist, followed by hints that they should now "go and do likewise." The fact is that the majority of the population, by temperament and inclination, shy away from aggressive people who lobby them for attention. Conversely, most people feel uncomfortable at the very thought of trying to sell someone something — let alone attempting to tamper with their worldview and belief system. If ordinary church people are to become excited about evangelism, they must be offered models that do not require them to act like highly extroverted lobbyists.

For some people, reluctance about evangelism is simply a matter of courage. They don't want to be thought of as different; they don't want to stand out. They would just like to blend in and be part of the crowd. This is perfectly natural. But it is important to remember that the calling of the Church and of Christians is to be salt and light in the world, not simply to blend in. As followers of Jesus, we have a high calling and a great responsibility. By definition, Christians stand apart; we are different. As the early Christians were reminded in the First Epistle of Peter, "You are a chosen race, a royal priesthood, a holy nation, God's own people, in order that you may proclaim the mighty acts of him who called you out of darkness into his marvelous light" (1 Peter 2:9).

Frequently, we lack confidence because we think we do not understand the Gospel well enough to share it properly. It is quite simply a fact that many people in mainline churches, after a lifetime of faithful attendance and committed service, do not feel that they have a clear understanding of what Christianity is really all about. They could not, if asked, write or explain clearly in one or two paragraphs the essence of the faith. Others are afraid that they will be asked difficult questions, for which they will not be able to provide answers.

Why this lack of confidence in our knowledge? We need to admit that our churches have not, on the whole, done a good job of teaching the faith or of helping adults grow into mature disciples of Jesus. Many people spend their entire lives in churches where the name of Jesus is never even mentioned outside the liturgy. For too long, we have settled for regular church attendance and volunteer service, without encouraging and enabling our members to grow towards spiritual maturity.

I frequently speak with people who have been committed participants in church life for years but who admit quite readily that they are not sure whether or not they are really Christians. In one case, a person said quite seriously, "I don't really know whether I'm a Christian, but I do know that I'm an Anglican." Is it any wonder that such people aren't all that eager to get involved in evangelism? They hope they are genuine Christians, but they have no sense of assurance. Lacking an adequate understanding of grace, many of them are simply trying to do their best, hoping that, in the end, when their lives are measured against some unknown standard, they will be found acceptable. These people have not been well served by the church.

Lack of knowledge and certainty among the laity may not be so surprising, for our seminaries have not generally taught the clergy how to make disciples of their congregations. Evangelism requires the difficult initial work of making mature disciples and equipping them for evangelism. But our clergy have not been taught how to make disciples, nor how to equip people for evangelism. It is a vicious circle, and only rarely is it broken.

We are part of a church structure that acts as though Christendom were still alive and well — that the majority of people are already Christians and that the work of the Church and its clergy is to provide worship services and pastoral care. But Christendom is dead, at least in this part of the world, and the Church is in a missionary situation. This calls for a radical refocusing of who we are and what we do as the Church.

Lack of Confidence in the Gospel
Some people in the Church have lost their confidence in the Gospel itself. In other words, they doubt whether the basic tenets of the faith are true and whether the Gospel does, in fact, have the power to lead people into a new life of reconciliation with God and passion for God's reign. I can think of at least three reasons for this. The first has to do with a lack of serious teaching and study (as just described). Discipleship does not come naturally, since the life of faith runs counter to our most basic instincts. Particularly in this secular society, where relativism is part of the air we breathe, we must work at our faith. With the gravitational pull of society towards relativism and cynicism, faith left untended will quickly atrophy and die. Clergy must reclaim their primary work of teaching the faith.

A second reason goes back to the current condition of the Church. Many people have spent their entire lives in churches that have never seen an adult conversion. When church life is all about running an organization and keeping it going, it easily degenerates into dull routine, with no surprises, no hint of the supernatural, no sense of spiritual awakening taking place in people's lives. Without the positive reinforcement of seeing that the Gospel actually does change people's lives for the better — and that people outside the faith are willing to engage in dialogue and even turn to Christ — it is only logical to begin to question whether what we claim is really true or just a nice idea that we happen to find attractive.

The third reason, I suggest, is that people become confused when they read books, articles, or interviews by church leaders who are questioning or even denying central tenets of the faith. To be sure, there is a place for constructive questioning and inquiry within the faith and there is a place for wrestling with doubt. But when those who are in positions of leadership publicly deny key tenets of Christianity, we can hardly blame laypeople for getting confused and lacking confidence.

Serious attention to the work of teaching and discipleship would go a long way towards offsetting this uncertainty. The people of God would then be well grounded in the faith and therefore in a better position to consider such statements in a thoughtful and informed manner. There is less chance that they would feel as though they were being blown around in a storm. Similarly, those who are privileged enough to share in the life of churches where people are routinely coming to faith will be less susceptible to the public undermining of the faith.

Once again, we come back to the primary work of making disciples. For evangelism to prosper, we need parish communities where the majority of people can say with St Paul, "I am not ashamed of the gospel; it is the power of God for salvation to everyone who has faith" (Romans 1:16), and who can meet the challenge in the First Epistle of Peter to "always be ready to make your defense to anyone who demands from you an accounting for the hope that is in you" (1 Peter 3:15).

The Challenge

There is an interesting story in the Book of Numbers (chapters 13 and 14) describing an incident that took place when the people of Israel were in the wilderness on their way from Egypt to Canaan. Moses sent twelve men into Canaan to check out the terrain and bring back an espionage report. When they returned, forty days later, they regaled the people with tales of the splendours of a land flowing with "milk and honey" (Numbers 13:27). But ten of the spies warned the Israelites that the cities were fortified and the Canaanites were so tall that the spies looked like grasshoppers compared to them. We will never be able to stand against the Canaanites, said the ten. Two of the spies were far more confident, however, and tried to remind the people that because God had promised to be with them, they would be more than equal to the challenge. But the people were intimidated by the first report, and lost heart. What could have been a great moment in their history turned out, instead, to be a long period of wandering aimlessly in the wilderness.

This story is an excellent model for our current situation. If we choose to focus on all the reasons why evangelism will be difficult, we will easily be intimidated and shrink from the challenge. But if, like the two faithful spies, we stay focused on our mission and remember that God is with us, we will experience the goodness and faithfulness of God. The secularism of this age has created a deep spiritual hunger in the land. The Church is poised on the threshold of a marvellous opportunity if only we will take it. Many of our congregations have been wandering in the wilderness far too long. Let us pray that God will give us the courage and the resolve to meet these challenges and to seize the opportunity before us with imagination, integrity, and anticipation. This is all part of the great adventure of discipleship.

CHAPTER FIVE

The Congregations We Need

In spite of many differences and concerns about the nature and practice of evangelism, I believe that most mainline Christians will agree on two key points. The first is that any healthy form of evangelism will emerge from the life of a faith community and that it will lead to new people being included in that community. In other words, evangelism should be firmly rooted in the life of a local church. Any evangelistic effort will be suspect if it seeks to avoid the life of the local faith community, if it does not have clear lines of accountability, or if it does not seek to bring people into active participation in the life and worship of a local congregation.

The second point is that evangelism and conversion should be thought of more as processes than as events. To be sure, there will be many significant events and turning points within the process, but conversion, properly understood, occurs over time. We will realize that it takes time to hear and consider the Gospel and to make the decision to turn to Christ. In our evangelistic efforts, we will insist that people be treated gently, with dignity and respect. We will not want to rush people, to treat them like targets or quotas. We will insist on giving them all the time and space they need, trusting that God's Spirit will work in God's time. We will be friends, guides, encouragers — not high-pressure salespeople.

The Community as Evangelist

One of the popular stereotypes of evangelism is that it is the exclusive preserve of a few highly extroverted and aggressive personalities. But evangelism at its very best is the work of the entire congregational community. This community might well (and ideally should) contain some extroverted and committed people who clearly have the unique gift of evangelism, but even these gifted evangelists will not be able to carry out their ministry effectively without the assistance of their entire congregation. It takes everyone working together as a team (or, in the language of St Paul, as a "body") for evangelism to be effective.

Central to this understanding of evangelism as the ministry of the whole congregation is a healthy, dynamic church community, whose members understand themselves to be "disciples-in-the-making" and who, as their faith grows and deepens, are eager to help others turn to Christ and learn to follow him. The members of such a church understand that, for them, Christian learning and growth never end. Through the ministry of their congregation, in its various forms, they are constantly being nurtured, strengthened, encouraged, and challenged to a deeper and broader understanding of their faith and its implications for daily life. As they live their lives in the places where their various relationships, responsibilities, and activities take them, they strive to remember that they do so as ambassadors of the reign of God and as witnesses to God's love and grace. They are learning to speak naturally and confidently, without embarrassment, about their faith and the life of their church. They readily invite those within their natural spheres of influence to come and sample the life of their church community.

Obviously, to make such invitations, they must be confident that those who accept will experience a grace-filled, loving community that welcomes newcomers warmly and offers them a place to belong. Within the loving, nurturing, healing environment of this community, sensitively, over time, these newcomers will learn of God's loving grace, and they will be invited to accept God's offer of reconciliation, forgiveness, and healing.

I am convinced that one of the key tasks of the leadership in any congregation is to hold continually before the members of that congregation the vision of their church becoming such a community, and then of nurturing that community into being. The magnitude of this challenge should not be underestimated.

Three Key Players

In this style of evangelism, in which the congregation as a whole is regarded as the primary evangelist, there are three key players, each of whom has a specific role to play. If any of these key players fail to do their part, nothing much can happen. If they work together, their congregation will almost inevitably have the joy of seeing many people come to a growing faith through their corporate ministry.

The first key player is the *senior minister* or the *leadership team* that has been entrusted with the leadership of the congregation. If a church is to have an effective ministry of evangelism, the leadership, especially the senior minister, must believe absolutely that God wants people to come to faith in Christ through the ministry of this church community, and that this can happen.

In addition to holding out the vision of such a community, the primary role of the senior minister or leadership team is to make provision for the work of teaching the faith and making disciples. If this work is neglected, the members of the congregation will not understand the importance of evangelism; nor will they feel that they have a faith that is worth sharing. They will only feel confused and vulnerable whenever they hear Church leaders talk about evangelism.

The second key player is the *congregation* as a whole. The role of the congregation is to become the type of community described above — a community in which the Gospel is both taught and lived and in which God's love, forgiveness, and healing grace can be experienced. If the congregation is not growing into such a community, the witness of evangelism will lack integrity. If we cannot invite people to experience the life of a grace-filled, welcoming, and healing community, our evangelism is little more than empty rhetoric.

The third key player is each *individual member* of the congregation. Their role is to network within their natural spheres of influence, welcoming opportunities to witness to their faith and inviting their friends and families to come and sample the life of their faith community. If this is neglected, the parish will quickly become ingrown and exclusive.

Each of these three partners is absolutely essential to the process of evangelism. If any one is missing, evangelistic efforts will fall flat. When all three are in place, good things will happen.

Strengths and Weaknesses

The strength of this form of evangelism is that it takes seriously the biblical concept of the Church as "the people of God." It rightly takes into account the fact that God's purposes in redemption do not begin or end with the individual. Throughout the Bible, God is always shown to have been in the process of forming a distinctive community of people who will live in the world as light in the darkness. In the New Testament, this community was the Church, and it still is today. The mission of the Church is to bear witness, through its life and worship, to the truth of the Gospel, to live as a sign and model of the reign of God, and to work for the reconciliation of the entire world to God through Jesus Christ. Individuals who are attracted by the life and witness of this community and who respond to the invitation of the Gospel become a part of the community, taking their place in its ongoing mission.

The most obvious weakness of this form of evangelism is, quite frankly, the present condition of many congregations. If we are to make progress in this important ministry of evangelism, we must be honest about this. Unfortunately, we cannot simply assume that the majority of our congregations are loving, welcoming communities, offering newcomers a grace-filled, healing, and nurturing environment in which to hear, experience, and consider the invitation of the Gospel. As Lee Strobel points out in his excellent book *Inside the Mind of Unchurched Harry and Mary*, "There's a good chance Harry would try church if a friend invited him — but this may actually do him more harm than good" (p. 79). Any congregation that wants to become an effective "evangelizing community" must begin by taking a long, hard look at itself.

For many mainline Christians, perhaps the first and greatest challenge will lie in making the necessary adjustments to begin thinking of their church as an evangelizing community. For many, this represents a radical change from their usual understanding of church life and ministry. The traditional form of parish ministry was shaped by the Church at a time when Christendom was still alive. By "Christendom" I mean that social and political climate, dominant in the West for the past fifteen centuries, in which it was assumed that the culture was Christian. In the days of Christendom, people thought of the phrases "good Christian" and "good citizen" as virtually synonymous; when someone said, "God," everyone understood what the word referred to.

In the days of Christendom, people naturally looked to the Church for answers to their spiritual and religious questions and expected the Church to provide its pastoral services and rites at the appropriate times and seasons. In such circumstances, the appropriate form of ministry in the local church was the pastoral mode, in which the priest or minister, trained in pastoral ministry, shepherded the "faithful flock" through life.

In the days of Christendom, the typical churchgoer, if asked about the purpose of the Church, would probably reply with something like "The church is where I go to worship God, and to have my spiritual needs met." If questioned further about his or her role in the ministry of the Church, the reply might well be, "The priests look after the ministry; I contribute my share of the financial costs, and help out on a committee or two around the church, as I have time." (In *The Once and Future Church*, Loren Mead describes in more detail the Church under Christendom.)

In Canada today, Christendom is dead. There is no longer a prevailing Christian worldview, nor a societal consensus that the Church is the primary broker of truth and values. The Church can no longer reasonably assume that the institutions and structures of society are its allies. They cannot be counted on to support the authority of the Church. In the days of post-Christendom, society challenges the Church. Where Christendom led people into the Church, post-Christendom leads them out. (This does not mean that post-Christendom is spiritually disinterested. On the contrary, there is a lively spiritual curiosity and interest within Canada. But there is no sense that the Church has a monopoly on such matters. Some even question whether it has anything at all to contribute to the discussion! The Church is regarded as just one voice among many in the marketplace of ideas, and some see it as an ineffective or suspect voice.)

In this radically changed situation, many churches are still attempting to work from the Christendom model. It is no wonder they are experiencing difficulty! In many cases, the harder they work, the more irrelevant they seem to become. It is not so much that what they have done in the past is wrong; it is simply that what they have done in the past is inappropriate in the present context. We cannot turn back the clock. We must accept that times have changed, and in order to minister effectively, our model for church life and for outreach to the community must change as well.

From Maintenance to Mission

This change of focus is currently being described as the shift from maintenance to mission. *Maintenance* describes the "business as usual" approach to ministry. The emphasis here is on maintaining the present forms and structures of ministry, emphasizing traditional forms of worship, with the parish priest providing pastoral care for the faithful. *Mission* describes an outwardly focused congregation, in which it is recognized that the Church is currently in a missionary situation. Rather than maintaining the traditional forms and structures and being content to minister to the faithful, the mission-minded church understands that a major part of its task is to share the Gospel with the unconverted, with the intention of encouraging them to accept God's offer of reconciliation and to share in the life of the people of God.

The contrast in thinking in these two types of congregation is like the difference between night and day. Consider the following points of comparison:

1. In measuring the *effectiveness*, the maintenance congregation asks, "How many pastoral visits are being made?"

The mission congregation asks, "How many disciples are being made?"

2. When contemplating some form of *change*, the maintenance congregation says, "If this proves upsetting to any of our members, we won't do it."

   The mission congregation says, "If this will help us reach someone on the outside, we will take the risk and do it."

3. When thinking about *change*, the majority of members in a maintenance congregation ask, "How will this *affect* me?"

   The majority of members in the mission congregation ask, "Will this *increase our ability to reach those outside?*"

4. When thinking of its *vision for ministry*, the maintenance congregation says, "We have to be faithful to our past."

   The mission congregation says, "We have to be faithful to our future."

5. The priest in the maintenance congregation says to the *newcomer*, "I'd like to introduce you to some of our members."

   In the mission congregation the members say, "We'd like to introduce you to our priest."

6. When confronted with a *legitimate pastoral concern*, the priest in the maintenance congregation asks, "How can I meet this need?"

   The priest in the mission congregation asks, "How can this need be met?"

7. The maintenance congregation *seeks to avoid conflict* at any cost (but rarely succeeds).

   The mission congregation understands that *conflict is the price of progress*, and is willing to pay the price. It understands that it cannot take everyone with it. This causes some grief, but it does not keep it from doing what needs to be done.

8. The *leadership style* in the maintenance congregation is primarily *managerial*, where leaders try to keep everything in order and running smoothly.

   The leadership style in a mission congregation is primarily *transformational*, casting a vision of what can be, and marching off the map in order to bring the vision into reality.

9. The maintenance congregation is concerned with the *Church*, its institutional nature, its organizations and structure, its canons and committees.

   The mission congregation is concerned with the *culture*, with understanding how secular people think and what makes them tick. It tries to determine their needs and their points of accessibility to the Gospel.

10. When thinking about *growth*, the maintenance congregation asks, "*How many Anglicans* live within our parish borders?"

    The mission congregation asks, "*How many unchurched people* live within a twenty-minute drive of this church?"

11. The maintenance congregation looks at the community and asks, "How can we *get these people to support the Church*?"

    The mission congregation asks, "How can the *Church support these people*?"

12. The maintenance congregation thinks about *how to save the Church*.

    The mission congregation thinks about *how to reach the world*.

Three Key Questions

A church that is interested in moving from maintenance to mission should ask itself the following three questions.

1. *What would we like to see happen in the lives of the people who come to join in the life of this congregation?* Until a congregation can answer this question clearly, it really has no business thinking about how to attract newcomers. Those who come within a church's sphere of ministry need to experience the reality of God's loving and healing grace incarnated in the life of the Christian community before they will eventually turn to Christ and become healthy, mature, holistic disciples. Any answer to the question that falls short of this is inadequate.

The mission of the Church is to make disciples whose lives, individually and corporately, bear witness to the reality of God's reign and the salvation God offers through Jesus Christ. The mission-minded church wishes this for everyone it seeks to reach; it also has a clear understanding of how it plans to accomplish this.

2. *What, from the point of view of those we would like to reach, would make this church a worthwhile community to join?* Most churches can readily think of a number of good reasons why they would like to have some new members join them, but these reasons wouldn't ordinarily engage the imaginations of the currently unchurched.

A mission-minded church is learning to think like the people it is trying to reach. It has the courage to look at itself honestly and ask what it has to offer that would make it worth the while of the currently unchurched to give up their Sunday morning routine and to join the church in worship. It realizes that if the honest answer is "not much," it has some serious work to do.

3. *What price are we as a congregation prepared to pay in order to reach and assimilate newcomers?* The mission-minded church realizes that there is a price to be paid for reaching out and welcoming new people. Newcomers bring new needs, new expectations, new demands. The

price of genuine evangelism is paid in terms of money, time, work, change, and, for those unwilling to pay the price in these categories, loss. But the mission-minded church quickly realizes that the price, however great, is well worth it for the joy of seeing the Gospel take root in the lives of those it reaches.

Five Key Areas of Congregational Life to Address

In order to lead a congregation along the continuum from a maintenance to a mission orientation, there are five key areas of congregational life to which the leadership must pay special attention. The first is not necessarily more important than the second or third, but the second follows more naturally when the first is in place, and the third when the second is in place, and so on.

1. Practise Transformational Leadership

There is a qualitative difference between being a manager and being a leader, and anyone seeking to help a congregation move from a maintenance to a mission orientation must know the difference. Managers are concerned with systems and routines, with making sure that things are organized and running smoothly. Leaders are concerned with developing a vision and leading their organization through the necessary processes of change in order to turn the vision into a reality. As some have said, "Managers do things the right way. Leaders do the right things." It is possible for a manager to become very efficient at doing the wrong things. When this happens, the whole organization suffers, in spite of the manager's efficiency. Every organization needs both management and leadership, but clergy who are seeking to refocus their churches for witness and growth must function primarily as leaders rather than as managers.

Leadership is about effecting change, but the type of change required in our congregations is transformational rather than merely reformational. Through reformational change, we seek better ways of doing what we are already doing. But we want to become something completely different; we want to become mission congregations. This requires transformational, not reformational, change.

Transformational leaders have a clear conviction that God can and will work through their congregation to change lives, and that their congregation of people can be used by God to help change the world. Such leadership begins with a clear vision of the evangelizing community, and what that community might look like in its particular setting and circumstances. It is able to initiate and manage constructive change, as it leads the congregation through the process of transition from maintenance to mission. Vision is absolutely key. Otherwise, people will think that the change is simply a matter of the leader's personal preference. This makes for reluctance in accepting the proposed changes.

The transformational leader teaches the congregation what it means to be the people of God, what their mission is, and how the suggested changes will make them more effective in this mission. Such a leader is able to motivate people to take risks and to give up their personal preferences for the greater sake of the mission. This type of leader understands the difference between the truly important and the merely urgent, and refuses to let the urgent deflect focus and energy from the important.

2. Reclaim the Ministry of Making Disciples

The first priority for any church seeking to become a genuinely evangelizing community is to reclaim the ministry of making disciples. If this is not done, nothing of any significance can happen through the life of that congregation. Unless this work of teaching the faith and equipping people for ministry is taken seriously, the people of the church will understand neither the urgency nor the rationale for evangelism.

It is undeniable that the call of the New Testament is for those who have turned to Christ as Saviour and Lord to grow to maturity in their faith. In his letter to the Colossians, St Paul writes, "It is he [Christ] whom we proclaim, warning everyone and teaching everyone in all wisdom, so that we may present everyone mature in Christ" (Colossians 1:28). The goal of the apostolic ministry was not simply to gain intellectual assent to the Gospel message, but to transform people who turned to Christ. The intent was to make disciples, nurturing individuals and congregations to spiritual maturity so that God's redeeming work could be done, not only in them but also through them.

It is fair to say that the primary measure of effectiveness of any church should be the cadre of disciples that it teaches, nurtures, equips, and deploys throughout society on a weekly basis to witness to God's grace in Jesus Christ and to pass on the Good News of God's reign. It is all too easy to lose sight of this and to rely on quite secular criteria as measures of effectiveness (for example, the number of people attending worship services, the sophistication of our liturgy, our financial situation, and so on). To be sure, these are important factors in the life of any congregation, but they are not the primary indicators of effectiveness.

It is also fair to say that generally we have ignored this important work of making disciples. This is probably a logical consequence of the Christendom mindset, in which it was assumed that all of life reinforced a Christian worldview and Christian thought and behaviour. Whatever its cause, it is a fact that many of our present members have no sense of growing as disciples. They do not think of the church primarily as a centre for mission, nor do they think of themselves as ambassadors for Christ in the places where they live and work.

In his book *Biblical Perspectives on Evangelism*, Walter Brueggemann suggests that those whom the church is seeking to evangelize fall into three major categories: *outsiders*, whom we want to help become insiders; *beloved children*, whom we want to help grow into belief-ful adults; and *forgetters*, whom we want to help become rememberers. The first two categories are perhaps more obvious than the third. The forgetters to whom he refers are current Church members who have forgotten (if they ever knew) what it means to be the people of God. He describes these "forgetters" as "insiders to the faith who have grown careless, weary, jaded, and cynical about the faith" (p. 71). Concerning these "forgetters," Bruegge-mann writes: "[E]vangelism is a task not simply of making outsiders into insiders, but of summoning insiders from amnesia to memory. I suspect that very many so-called insiders are in fact functional outsiders, 'alienated from the commonwealth of Israel,' i.e., completely cut off from the odd identity of covenant." He continues: "I believe that the reality of amnesia is massive among us. That amnesia (which on the surface shows up as 'illiteracy') causes the Church to lack in any serious missional energy" (p. 90).

We need to pay careful attention to Brueggemann's observations that "the evangelizing of insiders (i.e., most of the Western Church) may be our primary agenda in evangelism" (p. 73). From personal observation, I know that it is not at all uncommon to find people in our churches who have attended faithfully for years, who have worked hard for the church, who have given faithfully and generously of their time, energy, and money, but who would readily admit that they have only a very superficial understanding of what it is really all about.

Many church members are confused about the faith; others are plainly mistaken. For many, faith is a mixture of warm feelings and vague hopes, expressed in a rather quaint religious language. Many never use the name of Jesus outside of liturgy. People who do speak enthusiastically about Jesus are often regarded as an embarrassment.

It is worth noting here that not all such people are, in Brueggemann's words, "careless, weary, jaded, or cynical." Many are simply frustrated (and hence, perhaps on the way to becoming jaded or cynical) at the lack of help and direction they are receiving in their attempts to grow in their faith. Many of them are quite prepared to acknowledge that they do not know how to go about reading the Bible with a sense that they are doing so in a responsible way. Given the opportunity, they willingly share their frustration with their attempts to read the Bible on a regular basis, only to become quickly bogged down and discouraged, once again.

Many are equally prepared to acknowledge that they do not know how to pray. There are lifelong churchgoers who could not say a simple grace at a church dinner without asking for help. By far the majority of our members would not be comfortable praying aloud in a small group of their fellow parishioners, either for the ministry of their church or over some issue in the life of one of the members. They would simply not know how to do this. Yet it seems obvious from the New Testament that such prayer is a normal part of the Christian life.

Our weakness in making disciples is a major factor contributing to the current malaise of our Church. It certainly works against any enthusiasm for evangelism. How can people be excited at the prospect of trying to share a faith about which they themselves are confused? If we can't pray together, read the Scriptures, or talk about Jesus with one another, what hope do we have of bearing any effective witness to the reign of God in a secular world amongst people with little or no Christian memory? And if we have no clear sense of what it means to be the people of God — of what God intends the Church to be and to do — how can we organize our congregational life in such a way as to carry out our mission faithfully, effectively, and joyfully?

The way forward lies in acknowledging our complacency in this area and reaffirming that the primary work of the Church is the making of mature disciples who, in their daily life and work, understand themselves to be fully devoted followers of Jesus and ambassadors for the reign of God. Everything else we do is a function of this.

To the degree that we are able to reclaim the ministry of making disciples, teaching the faith, and equipping people to live it faithfully, enthusiastically, and consistently, we have a hope of turning our churches around. And wherever any congregation begins to work seriously at making mature disciples of its members, there will be an accompanying enthusiasm for evangelism as well. In my book *Following Jesus: First Steps on the Way*, I seek to offer practical help in this area, focusing on six areas of teaching and practice that must be emphasized for healthy growth in discipleship.

3. Help Your Congregation Become a Community

As a church focuses on making disciples, its discipleship training will include an emphasis on the importance of building community. Unfortunately, we know only too well that we cannot simply assume that a congregation is automatically a community. Congregation and community are not synonyms. There is more to Christian community than simply gathering with other like-minded people to participate in a service of worship. Yet it is obvious that a congregation cannot become an evangelizing community unless it is first of all a community. If people are going to invite their friends to hear and experience the Gospel through their church, they must be confident that when their friends come, they will find a warm and vibrant Christian community eager to welcome and accept them.

Christian community is formed at the foot of the cross, with the acknowledgement that we are all equally in need of God's grace. We come to the cross with our own particular expressions of need and brokenness, confident that Christ will accept us and do a work of grace in our lives. Because Christ accepts and forgives us, we accept one another.

Growing Christians realize the importance of Jesus' words that it is through the way they love one another that they will be recognized by the world as his followers (John 13:34–35). They understand that the quality of their corporate life is a sign of the reconciling work of Christ in their lives. As a Christian community, a significant part of their mission is to model in their common life the reconciliation that is proclaimed in the Gospel.

But community is not created simply by talking about how important it is. Congregational leaders seeking to lead their congregations through the transformation from maintenance to mission must work consciously and consistently to foster the emergence of community life. This begins by creating simple and safe opportunities for people just to get to know one another. They need chances to talk about themselves, about their lives, where they work, where they grew up, the things they enjoy, and so on. Good conversations can often take place over meals. I have never yet seen a congregation that couldn't use a few more good parties, just to help the members get to know one another better.

People also need opportunities to share their faith stories with one another. Community is deepened when people begin to speak openly with one another about their personal faith histories. The stories of their first experiences in church, of their earliest understandings of themselves as Christians, of their growing understanding of the Gospel, of the people who have had the greatest influence in their Christian commitment and faith development — these things provide fascinating listening and forge strong bonds as they are shared. (Such conversations are also essential in developing a person's confidence in speaking about his or her faith with those who are not currently believers.)

As community slowly develops, people will begin to trust one another and understand that they are in a safe place. This opens the door to sharing areas of their lives where they feel the most vulnerable. They will be able to speak of their weaknesses, their doubts, their temptations, their frustrations, and their failures. They will be able to ask one another for help, for encouragement, for prayer. This level of trust is built slowly, only in smaller groups, and only when people have come to know each other through more general, less threatening types of sharing. But when it begins to happen, it is a sure sign that what was once a congregation is beginning to become a true community — a safe, caring, healing community into which the members will be pleased to invite their friends.

4. Give Pastoral Care Back to the People
When I speak to clergy about the priority of teaching the faith and making disciples, I sometimes see a glazed look in their eyes. I can almost read their thoughts: "Where do you think I'm going to find time for that? I'm already running around like a madman trying to take care of everyone in the church!" And that is the problem! One of the great reversals that needs to take place in our churches is for the clergy to give the pastoral care back to the people. This not only gives the clergy the time they need for the work of teaching and equipping; it also makes for better pastoral care in many (if not most) cases.

The first objection I usually hear to this somewhat radical suggestion is: "The people in my church wouldn't stand for it; they want their pastoral care from the minister." To the degree that this is true (and I don't doubt that it is), there are two key reasons. The first is that the people have not been properly discipled and therefore do not have a clear understanding of what the Church is all about. They are still operating from a Christendom mindset. That is why I emphasize again and again that the first priority is to make disciples. When this is happening, many other problems begin to be sorted out.

The second reason for this objection is that time has not been spent in building a deeply bonded Christian community. The people have not experienced the type of community described above, where they are able to share with one another at the deepest levels, confident that they will be accepted and cared for by one another when they do. It is not enough simply to hand off pastoral ministry. It must be done in the context of a bonded, caring community.

Every Christian congregation has within its membership almost unlimited potential for the ministry of caring. People simply love to be able to help one another; this is part of being human. Some people positively ache for the opportunity to be able to care for others in meaningful ways. The tragedy, indeed the scandal, is that in many of our churches these gifts lie untapped, while a single cleric runs around trying to have meaningful, caring relationships with an entire congregation. This is madness.

To paraphrase Woody Allen, 90 percent of pastoral care is simply showing up. I remember visiting a man in hospital who said to me, "You've got it made in this work. You're a winner the minute you walk through the door, just for coming to visit. As long as you don't say or do anything stupid while you're here, you can't lose." Of course, there is more to it than this. (In the New Testament church, pastoring was considered such an important ministry that only people like Stephen, full of the Spirit and wisdom, were appointed to the task [Acts 6:2–3].) Nevertheless, with a modicum of training, by far the greatest percentage of pastoral care in any parish could easily be handed over to a group of competent caregivers. My personal experience has been that, when this is done in the context of a disciple-making, bonding community, it invariably energizes the life and witness of that congregation.

5. Develop Celebratory Worship

A cartoon in a church publication showed a minister being led to the gallows to be hanged. A concerned church member was saying to the person beside him, "I tried to warn him not to change the order of the service." Tampering with set forms and styles of worship is a contentious and explosive issue in many congregations. Yet if a congregation is serious about becoming an evangelizing community, it must be prepared to examine this area of its life with openness and honesty. For most people, the worship service is the door through which they enter the church. When people are invited by a friend or when they decide on their own to investigate Christianity through their neighbourhood church, their first experience is usually a worship service.

Many longtime churchgoers have long since lost any sense of what their worship looks and feels like to newcomers. Many don't even wonder about this. Yet time and again, in conversations about the faith, people who do not attend church cite boredom with the services as a primary reason. Any congregation that is serious about reaching people for Christ must therefore have the courage to examine this area of its life honestly and ruthlessly. Every part of the worship service must be looked at. We must be aware of the importance of *music* — especially to those under forty years of age. For those of the Baby Boom generation and under, music is an essential part of the way they think and interact with life. If the music in the service is dull and lifeless, they will be gone before we ever have a chance to share the Gospel with them.

Similarly, the *sermons* must focus on practical applications to everyday life. People investigating the faith are not particularly interested in the preacher's personal political opinions or pet projects and organizations. They want to know whether Christianity makes sense, whether it will help them make sense of their lives, and whether the preacher is able to share with them some good news from God.

The renewal of worship is a topic that deserves its own book. Here I simply want to make the point that if the way we worship is a major obstacle to outsiders coming to faith, then how acceptable to God can our worship be? In the evangelizing congregation, worship services are planned with newcomers and outsiders to the faith in mind.

Because worship is the "front door" experience for many people coming to the church to consider Christianity, arguably this section on celebratory worship should be at the top of the list. But I have placed it here because the type of worship I am referring to grows out of the other considerations. Dynamic worship grows out of, and is a consequence of, a growing faith and a genuine community in which people are sharing their lives and caring for one another in deep and meaningful ways.

There are no techniques to make worship "come alive." Without growing faith and true community, our efforts to revitalize worship will amount to little more than obvious manipulation. I am convinced that we should be constantly working on our forms of music and worship texts, seeking to make them more accessible to new generations and to those outside the faith. However, I am equally persuaded that vitality in worship has little to do with whether we are using an ancient or contemporary rite, or whether we are singing old hymns or more modern compositions. These issues are not inconsequential, but they are not primary either. The most important question is whether or not the worshippers are truly experiencing God's presence among them.

This dynamism cannot be created on its own. It is a consequence of these other considerations. Newcomers to such a service of worship will inevitably remark, "There is something different about this church; I can't quite put my finger on it, but I know I can sense it." Hopefully, as they return again and again, they will find the words to describe what they have sensed: "Surely God is in this place."

Pray without Ceasing

This process of becoming an evangelizing community must be saturated with prayer. The church that is truly seeking to push back the darkness, to help people turn to the light, to empower people to renounce evil and embrace Christ, will find itself caught up in intense spiritual warfare. The members of such a congregation, having been taught to pray, will constantly ask for God's protection and guidance as they seek to win those to whom God is leading them. Such a congregation understands that without the power unleashed by prayer, their efforts will accomplish little of ultimate significance.

CHAPTER SIX

My Role in Evangelism

Evangelists and Witnesses

For many of us, our first reaction to the suggestion that we might have a significant role to play in the ministry of evangelism is one of disbelief. "What?" we exclaim. "Me, an evangelist? You must be joking!" Well, maybe; maybe not. The important thing to understand here is that the work of evangelism is not the exclusive preserve of those who have been gifted and called as evangelists. While recognizing their importance in the great enterprise of proclaiming the Good News and influencing others to become followers of Jesus, the New Testament also speaks of another important role in this ministry: the role of witnesses.

It is a major assumption of the New Testament that we are all witnesses. If you are an intentionally committed follower of Jesus, seeking to grow in your faith and to live the life of God's kingdom ever more faithfully, God wants to use you to influence others towards faith in Jesus and the life of the kingdom.

Those who are gifted evangelists sense that they have a special ability and desire for this ministry. Obviously, such people do not need to be convinced of the importance of evangelism. They need only to be given some elementary skills and pointed in the right direction. They seem to have a special talent for sniffing out evangelizing opportunities and for taking the initiative in developing evangelizing conversations. Many are able to debate, question, and persuade in such a way that people do not take offence, and many can point to a significant company of people whom they have helped become followers of Jesus. These people love evangelism; in fact, they live for it.

But not all of us, in fact not even the majority of us, are gifted in this way. Most of us sense that our primary gifts for ministry lie in other areas. Nevertheless, as committed followers of Jesus, it is important that we recognize the important role we have in witnessing to the Good News of what God has done in Jesus and to the reality of God's reign. In order to become effective witnesses in influencing others towards Jesus, it is not necessary that we put life on hold while we study for a doctorate in theology or develop the final answers to the many and varied questions that people might ask us about God and the spiritual life.

The role of a witness, quite simply, is to describe what one has seen, heard, or experienced. Others are then able to draw their own conclusions from the testimony of the witness. They will ask themselves if they consider this witness to be credible, if the testimony makes sense, and if it squares with what they have heard from other witnesses. An effective witness is not necessarily one who is a skilful speaker or a persuasive debater. The most effective witness is one who is able to describe accurately and confidently what happened, from his or her point of view.

One of my favourite examples of a witness in the New Testament is the blind man we read about in chapter 9 of John's Gospel. This man's sight was restored by Jesus, but because the healing took place on the Sabbath, he soon found himself being scrutinized by the religious authorities. This poor man was no match for the educated elite and was unable to respond to their questions in a satisfactory way. Finally, in exasperation, he blurted out, "One thing I do know, that though I was blind, now I see" (John 9:25). Now that is an effective witness.

Ability *vs.* Availability

In a society that rightly values pluralism and that moves so easily from pluralism to relativism, it is essential that we keep reminding ourselves about the importance of evangelism. Otherwise, it is almost inevitable that we will give in to the spirit of the age and begin to ask why we should even bother trying to influence others towards Jesus. Why not just leave them alone? God's people should never underestimate the high-powered seduction of secularism.

In chapter 1, we explored some of the reasons why evangelism is important and why we should be concerned with bringing this ministry back into the centre of the life of our churches. But if this is going to happen on any significant scale, it is important that we understand the importance of a good attitude towards this ministry and a healthy motivation to embark on it. Why should I personally be interested in this ministry? Why should I be willing to take some degree of responsibility for ensuring that it is given its rightful place in my church? Why should I personally take the time and make the effort to become an intentional witness within my personal spheres of influence?

These are foundational questions. Ultimately they are far more important than the question of how evangelism can be done sensitively and graciously. Do I want to become an effective witness? Would I like to influence others towards Jesus? Am I willing to put some serious work into becoming a faithful and effective witness? Without a high degree of motivation and desire, the question of how to do it is really not an issue. As is so often the case in the Christian life, the question of our availability is initially far more important than the question of our ability.

As I see it, there are three considerations that play a major role in developing a healthy motivation to begin evangelizing. These are astonishment, confidence, and faithfulness.

Astonishment

The absolute key to healthy motivation for evangelism, I believe, is a sense of genuine astonishment at God's grace to us in Jesus Christ. The most eager and passionate evangelists and witnesses must surely be those who have thought long and deep about the love and grace that lies behind the story of Jesus, and who have been completely overwhelmed by the searching, seeking, and saving love of God expressed at such cost in the incarnation, crucifixion, and resurrection.

This sense of astonishment breaks through in the First Letter of John as the writer exclaims, "See what love the Father has given us, that we should be called children of God; and that is what we are" (1 John 3:1). St Paul, the former persecutor of those who followed Jesus, knew it too, and expressed his astonishment in his epistle to the Romans (Romans 5:6–8).

One of the unfortunate marvels of human nature is our capacity to become jaded with the story of Jesus and of God's unceasing love for us. I once heard a speaker remark, somewhat cynically, that every week an incredible miracle takes place in churches all over North America. Preachers, he said, take the greatest story ever told and manage to bore people to tears with it.

Unless our efforts are inspired by the astonishment at the Gospel and at what God's grace has done for us personally, witnessing and evangelizing, if done at all, will be little more than a dreary religious duty and will bear little fruit.

Confidence

The second key to a healthy motivation for evangelism is a sense of confidence in the Gospel itself. Christian people individually, and churches collectively, that have lost their confidence in the power of the Gospel to change lives, can hardly be expected to be enthusiastic about the prospect of seeking to influence others to become followers of Jesus. Without such confidence, it just won't happen. Christianity will only be seen as something for "those who are inclined that way" or "who go in for that sort of thing."

Frequently, when conducting workshops on evangelism, I have pointed out to the participants that when we read a good book, watch a good movie, or find a good restaurant, we are eager to share this information with a friend. Why, then, I ask, do you think we are so reluctant to invite friends to join us when we find a good church? The immediate and unanimous response to this line of questioning is that in sharing the news of a book, movie, or restaurant, our friends understand that we are attempting to add value or enjoyment to their lives. But there is a fear that an invitation to church might be perceived as a judgement on them. They may infer that there is something wrong with their lifestyle.

There are two errors that need to be corrected in this line of thinking. The first is that in sharing our faith or inviting a friend to accompany us to church (with the hope that they will return, and over time be evangelized through the life and witness of the congregation), we are not offering them something of value. This has everything to do with our confidence in the Gospel — a confidence that stems from our astonishment at what the Gospel is all about. It also comes from our personal experience and appreciation of God's grace in our own lives. In this sense, our attitude towards evangelism is a reliable indicator of our own spiritual health. Eventually, it all comes down to what we ourselves have experienced and what our faith in Jesus Christ means to us.

We need to think deeply and carefully about this until we know how our professed beliefs actually make a significant difference in our lives. Effective witnessing requires a sense of confidence that this is an act of genuine friendship, because it is a serious attempt to enrich the life of the friend with whom we are sharing. We must truly believe that the Gospel is good news!

The second error in this line of thinking lies in the assumption that, by encouraging someone to become a follower of Jesus, we think there is something wrong with that person. In inviting a friend to church, or in sharing our faith with another, we should be careful not to imply that there is something bad or morally defective about that person. Following Jesus is not primarily about being good or bad. We all know many wonderful people who are not professing Christians!

The fear that sharing faith implies a perceived moral defect is a residue of Christendom thinking, in which it was assumed that we live in a Christian culture, and the phrases "good Christian," "good person," and "good citizen" all meant the same thing. Christendom is over in North America, and we all recognize immediately that these three phrases are not synonymous. Many good people and good citizens are not professing Christians and would resent the implication that because of their morally upright and responsible lifestyles they should be considered Christians.

Following Jesus is not primarily about being good or bad, although as we grow towards maturity in our faith we should certainly be becoming "better" people. This is because the goal of our faith, on the level of personal character and behaviour, is to become like Jesus. But following Jesus is primarily about allegiance. It is a matter of where our heart is, where our loyalty is, of recognizing that we have chosen the life of God's kingdom, as proclaimed by Jesus and taught by the Bible, over against all the alternatives that are available to us.

We have chosen to follow Jesus because of our conviction that Jesus is the key to knowing God. In Jesus, we learn the truth we need to know about God and about ourselves. In Jesus, we have the Saviour we need, the only one who can rescue us from the power of evil and make it possible for us to recognize, choose, turn, and enter God's kingdom and begin learning to live the kingdom life. Do we think that all those who do not follow Jesus are morally defective? Of course not. Do we believe that it is important for them to know about Jesus and to have the opportunity to choose to follow him? Having tasted of God's grace for ourselves, how could we not?

Faithfulness

I am always amazed when I hear Christian people, and particularly church leaders, profess that they are not particularly interested in evangelism. My astonishment lies in the fact that Jesus, whom we profess to be following, and whom church leaders are supposedly encouraging and enabling those in their care to follow, was by his own admission first and foremost an evangelist. His own description of his ministry was this: "The Son of Man came to seek out and to save the lost" (Luke 19:10).

At the beginning of his public ministry, Jesus, perhaps with a touch of delicious irony, called a small group of fishermen to leave their work and follow him. You can almost see the gleam in his eyes as he tells them that he will teach them to fish for people (Matthew 4:18–33; Mark 1:16–20).

Matthew's Gospel closes with Jesus' final instructions to the disciples. Known as the Great Commission, the final verses of this account of Jesus' earthly ministry read:

> And Jesus came and said to them, "All authority in heaven and on earth has been given to me. Go therefore and make disciples of all nations, baptizing them in the name of the Father and of the Son and of the Holy Spirit, and teaching them to obey everything that I have commanded you. And remember, I am with you always, to the end of the age" (Matthew 28:18–20).

In his book *The Vital Congregation*, church consultant Herb Miller describes these statements from the opening and closing of Jesus' public ministry as the "bookends of Jesus' ministry." Since these statements open and close Matthew's record of his ministry and since all four Gospels describe Jesus doing the work of evangelism — proclaiming the kingdom powerfully both in word and in deed — it is difficult to shake the impression that evangelism is important to Jesus. It is obviously so central to his ministry that even a careful writer like Miller is prepared to say: "If you are not interested in evangelism, you had better check to see who you are following. There is a good chance that it is not Jesus" (p. 74).

As followers of Jesus, it is important to ask on a regular basis, "Where is he leading us?" Of course, he is leading us into the family of God or into the community of the people of God. And the biblical witness is clear that he is leading us home to heaven. But equally important, he is leading us into the world, where our mission is to represent him well to others and to share the Good News of the Kingdom, in word and in deed, in his name.

Frequently, those who cynically equate evangelism with what they regard as an unethical or distasteful interest in "numbers" are heard to remark, "Numbers don't matter; what matters is faithfulness." Of course, this is true. But the question remains — faithfulness to what, or to whom? Evangelism was of primary importance to Jesus. It goes without saying that it should also be of primary importance to those who claim to be his followers. The commitment to follow Jesus is itself a commitment to evangelism. The example and the instructions of Jesus should be the only motivation his followers really need.

In his book *Won by One*, the British priest and evangelism trainer Geoffrey Willis tells a lovely story that puts this whole issue of sharing our faith into its proper perspective. At the conclusion of a presentation to a group of church leaders on the subject of evangelism, a woman in the audience spoke up and said, "What you have been saying all comes down to two questions, doesn't it, really? Do you have a faith worth sharing? And do you have a friend worth sharing it with?" (p. x). I doubt that it is possible to state the issue more clearly than this.

Think of Yourself as an Influencer

As you think about what it would mean in your particular situation to become an effective Christian witness, perhaps the best advice I can give you is to think of yourself as a potential influencer. We noted earlier that evangelism is more a process than it is an event, and it is probably helpful for you to think of yourself as one link in the long chain or process through which one eventually turns to Christ and becomes an intentional disciple.

John Bowen, an evangelist to university students with InterVarsity Christian Fellowship of Canada, uses a simple but helpful visual aid in explaining this process. It is described in the Fall 1995 issue of the quarterly newsletter *Good Idea*. "Put it this way," Bowen writes. "Suppose that, in terms of their getting to know God, everyone in the world is on a continuum of 1 to 100:

1 _____ 50 _____ 100

No one is at zero, because, having been created in God's image, everyone knows at least something about God. Likewise, nobody is at 100, because no one knows God fully. Suppose that 50 is the point at which a person realizes how Jesus is the key to getting to know God, and they commit their lives to following him."

"Real evangelism, I contend," says Bowen, "is helping a person move along the scale in the right direction. Much evangelistic effort goes into trying to get people to cross the line from 49 to 51, and, clearly, that is important. Equally clearly, however, there is little point in hammering away at 49 if the person is only at 17."

John Bowen is absolutely right in this. The work of evangelism and of pre-evangelism is a seamless robe. Before farmers can plant seeds and hope to harvest a crop, they must prepare the soil. If they neglect this difficult preparatory work, they will expend a lot of energy in vain. We made the point earlier that the goal of evangelism is mature, healthy, holistic discipleship. But in helping people make the commitment to follow Jesus and become mature disciples, we must begin with them exactly where they are. Indispensable to this process are convinced and passionate witnesses who are willing to share what God has done in their lives with those who are still seeking. So think of yourself as a witness who is helping influence others towards Jesus. Your willingness to witness might prove to be a pivotal point in the process of someone eventually turning to follow Jesus.

Becoming a Good Witness

Many of us have been shaped in a spiritual tradition that has led us to view our faith as a private matter — not really a proper topic of conversation. Many others of us have spent our lives in churches where we have never been actively encouraged to share our faith. Only a few of us have likely been involved in churches that have given us practical help in learning how to speak of our beliefs.

Here, as in so many other areas of life and faith, the key to improvement and developing confidence is preparation and practice. Highly skilled athletes do not suddenly appear out of nowhere, performing their incredible feats of athletic prowess. Behind their apparently effortless grace, we know, lies a lifetime of dedication and hard work. We also know that they do not stop practising once they have made it to the top. For every hour they appear before the crowds in competition, they have spent many hours practising and preparing.

God will use you to influence others towards Jesus, within your spheres of influence. But it takes some work. Witnessing is a faith skill, just like Bible reading, prayer, pastoral care, worship, and stewardship. We won't all become world famous evangelists (nor, of course, would we want to) but we can all become effective witnesses, and we should want to.

God's Story and Your Story

In order to become an effective witness, there are two stories that you will need to know. The first is the biblical story, the second is your personal story. In workshops on evangelism, I sometimes describe these stories as "You in God's Story" and "God in Your Story." Many people balk here because they lack confidence in their knowledge of either story. But by making the effort, you can begin to understand both stories more clearly and deeply — and to the degree that you do, your life (and the lives of those you influence) will be enriched by them.

The biblical story is the story of God's proactive involvement in the affairs of this world, beginning with the story of creation and reaching its climax in the life, death, and resurrection of Jesus, who represents God's ultimate intervention in the affairs of this world. This is the story that is told in Scripture, and which is outlined so succinctly in our creeds and eucharistic prayers. Above all, it is the story of God's unstoppable love and absolute refusal to abandon us to the horrors of evil; it is the story of God seeking to rescue us even when we don't want to be rescued and God's desire to win our hearts and allegiance even when our affections are set on lesser gods.

You don't need to have mastered this story in all its details in order to be an effective witness, and much of the account would never even come up in a faith-sharing conversation. But the accounts of Jesus and the Church in the New Testament are God's response to the story begun in the Old Testament, and as God's people, we should be constantly seeking to improve our grasp of the whole story. It follows, then, that we need to spend regular time, preferably on a daily basis, reading and reflecting on Scripture. We need also to meet on a regular basis with like-minded Christians in order to reflect on our reading, to share our insights with one another, and to encourage one another to continued growth and faithfulness. In this way we will come to know God better, we will understand the Gospel better, and coincidentally, we will become more confident witnesses.

Your personal story is the story of your own faith development and experience of God's grace. The initial response of most people at this point is to dismiss their own stories as ordinary, uneventful, and therefore uninteresting. "My story," we think, "could not possibly be of interest to anyone but me, and it could certainly never be influential in helping someone else become a follower of Jesus."

But wait, think about this for a minute. How did you get to the point in your life where you are reading through the sixth chapter of a book about evangelism? Surely this in itself puts you in rather exclusive company! How did you get here? Think backwards and see where the trail takes you.

What influences have brought you to the point where you are interested in sharing your faith, or have at least developed an interest in thinking seriously about evangelism? What has made you wonder whether you or your church should be doing something about it? What key people have influenced your faith development? Who have your teachers been? Who have been your models and encouragers?

Have there been significant turning points in your spiritual journey? Are there people, circumstances, events that you can recall as having been significant factors in your becoming the Christian you are today? Have there been times when you have had an overpowering experience of God's presence with you? Have you discovered inner resources you didn't imagine you had that have helped you through difficult times? Have there been seemingly chance encounters, casual conversations, apparently insignificant choices and decisions that in hindsight turn out to have been pivotal events?

Are you able to put together the outlines of a preliminary "personal testimony" of faith? Is your story such that you can describe the process by which you came to know Jesus? (How did you eventually make the decision to follow him? Can you say what this choice and direction for your life has meant to you? What were you like before?

What first attracted you to Jesus? What made you want to follow him? How has this choice changed you?) Or is your story more one of a continual development, in which you have always known about Jesus and can never remember a time when you didn't count yourself among his followers? Either way, what is the good news about Jesus that you have experienced and that you would like to share?

Take some time to think about the story. Outline it, map it, or even draw it. Include the highs and the lows, the times of spiritual richness and the times that were more like a wilderness experience. Then share it with a friend. Perhaps it is better in the beginning to share it with a Christian friend. You will find this to be a great encouragement and a wonderful confidence booster as you prepare yourself to become a better witness.

There are two things I know about this. The first is that no matter what its shape and outline might be, you have a story that is worth sharing. You will be amazed at the richness and depth of your story if you take even just one hour to begin this process and to share your preliminary findings with a friend. The second is that people will be interested in hearing your story, and many will delight in it. People are naturally interested in one another. We love to learn the details of one another's lives. Too often our conversation remains superficial and never really reaches to this deeply personal level of sharing our spiritual interests and concerns.

I have led many people through this exercise in courses, workshops, and seminars, and I have always been astonished at what happens. The room becomes positively animated as the participants begin to share their "ordinary" stories with each other. But beyond this, a "holy presence" pervades the room, and no one is in any doubt that God is among them as they share. This "practice" among Christians is great preparation for witnessing to those currently outside the circle of faith. It convinces you that you do have something to say after all, and that what you have to say is authentic and interesting. If shared sensitively but with conviction, and at the appropriate time, you can be sure that those who are not yet Christians will find it interesting as well. God simply does not write boring stories! As you share with them, God will be there too. And God will be pleased to honour your faithfulness and to use your "ordinary" story to influence others towards faith.

CHAPTER SEVEN

Getting Started

In thinking about our personal role in the ministry of evangelism, perhaps the most important question is "Where do I start?" The simplest and most obvious answer to this question is: "Start within your natural spheres of influence." Most of us already have many relationships that offer ready-made opportunities for evangelizing conversations. We simply need to become more intentional about recognizing and taking advantage of the opportunities that are already there.

The initial challenge here for many of us might simply be to acknowledge that conversation about faith and spiritual issues are perfectly normal. Do not be fooled or intimidated by the deeply entrenched secularism of our age. The simple truth is that we live in a time of intense spiritual hunger and curiosity. We are surrounded by people who long for a deeper spiritual reality than they are currently experiencing. Jesus once told his disciples that the fields are ripe for the harvest. Those words are as true today in your neighbourhood as they were when Jesus spoke them in their original setting.

Spheres of Influence

The three most natural spheres of influence most of us have are family, work, and neighbourhood. In thinking about the people we might be able to influence towards faith, these three areas are probably the most obvious place to begin. It is within these spheres that we should be thinking about how we might become more intentional in seeking out and creating opportunities for faith-related conversations.

Think about where you live, where you work, and where you play. Who do you know in each of these facets of your life? What kind of relationships do you have with them? Do you know people who are currently outside the faith or who have no active involvement in the life of any church? Are you on friendly enough terms with any of them that you could initiate a faith-related conversation should the opportunity arise?

It might be helpful for you to draw three circles on a piece of paper, each circle representing one of these spheres. Inside the circle list the names of the people with whom you have regular contact within that sphere. Don't be hasty about this. Do it carefully, thoughtfully, thoroughly. How well do you know these people? What is the nature of your relationship with them? What do you know about them? Do you know about the circumstances of their lives? Do you know their interests, their fears, any of the problems they might be facing? Do you know anything about their church involvement or their attitude towards Christianity?

When you have a number of names in each circle, take some time to pray. Not just a short, perfunctory prayer, but one in which you ask God for guidance and discernment. Each day, for several days, pray about these lists. Ask God if there are people named in any of your lists whose hearts are being prepared for a faith conversation. The assumption here is that God is already at work in the world, preparing people to respond to the good news and to turn to follow Jesus. Without this assumption, evangelism is just an exercise in propaganda, and probably in futility as well. But when we make ourselves available for the ministry of witness and evangelism, we can be confident that God is already working in the lives of people we know and that we are being invited to share in this work. As we pray over these lists, we are asking God to direct us to the people whom he is preparing. Working with God in this way is what makes evangelism so exciting!

Every day, make time to pray quite specifically over these lists, asking God to direct you towards those whose hearts are being prepared to give the Gospel a hearing. See if one or two or three names begin to stand out from these lists for you. As they do, begin to think about how you might become proactive in engaging these people in faith-related conversations. These are the people with whom you should begin. You now know where to start.

Operation Andrew

Organizations that specialize in training for evangelism often encourage people to make an "Operation Andrew" List. Andrew was the brother of Simon Peter; the first chapter of John's Gospel tells how he met Jesus. "He first found his brother Simon," we read in verse 41, "and said to him, 'We have found the Messiah' (which is translated Anointed). He brought Simon to Jesus." An Operation Andrew List is a list of those people whom you would like to introduce to Jesus, just as Andrew did with his brother Peter. At the very least, you would like to have a part in helping to influence them towards faith. The names that stood out for you as you prayed over your lists should be the first names on your Operation Andrew List.

A short while ago, a middle-aged businessman began attending my church. Gary introduced himself to me as a "brand-new Christian," and I learned that he had recently made the decision to become a follower of Jesus. He had not had any particular interest in Christianity, but a business colleague whom he respected had been quite open about his faith with him, had initiated several faith-related conversations in an unobtrusive way, and had invited him to several functions to listen to Christian businesspeople talk about their faith. Gary listened and watched for a long time, gave it careful consideration, and eventually opened his life to Christ. For him, this was a powerful conversion experience.

One day, as we sat talking about evangelism in our church, we were discussing the possibility of encouraging our parishioners to begin an Operation Andrew List. I raised the question of how effective such lists might be, and Gary replied, "The friend whose witness brought me to Christ had my name on his Operation Andrew List for five years."

Think about that — an ordinary businessman, going about his life in everyday fashion, but seeking to be faithful and intentional in the ministry of witness and evangelism. He placed a colleague's name on his Operation Andrew List and began to pray for him every day. He prayed that God would prepare his friend's heart to be open to the Gospel, he prayed for opportunities to share his faith and to introduce his friend to Christ, he prayed that he would know what to say when the opportunities arose, and he prayed for the courage to take advantage of the opportunities that came. Five years later, he saw his friend converted.

So I asked Gary, "Do you resent the fact that your friend put your name on a list and prayed for you?" He looked surprised at the question, then smiled. "Not at all," he replied. "As a matter of fact, I thank God for him every day!" This "brand-new Christian" has grown quickly in his faith and is now a small group leader in our church.

In addition to the intentionality and focus of Gary's friend in his commitment to evangelism, this story illustrates two important evangelism principles. The first is that conversion is almost always a long process. This means that effective evangelism is not a hit-and-run affair. People need time to ask their questions, to think seriously about who they are and what they are living for. They need time to consider their options and to think about what it is they are committing themselves to should they decide to follow Jesus. Even in cases where conversion seems to be an instantaneous event, closer inspection will almost inevitably reveal that it is really a dramatic point in a process that has been going on for a long time.

The second principle arises naturally from the first. The process of conversion is almost always influenced by close friendships. Whenever surveys are conducted of the means through which people made the decision to turn to Christ, the results are similar. Usually, over 90 percent of the respondents indicate that their conversion was due primarily to, or at the very least was heavily influenced by, a close friend or family member who took an evangelizing interest in them. People are more open to being influenced by those they love and trust than by strangers. Before we get way off track thinking about how we can engage total strangers in faith conversations, we should be putting our efforts into thinking about how we can engage those with whom we already have healthy relationships.

What Should I Say?

Our ultimate goal in evangelism is that the person we are speaking to will eventually become a fully committed follower of Jesus Christ and a mature disciple. Evangelism is the part of the process in which we seek to encourage these future disciples to make the initial commitment to become followers of Jesus. It is important to keep in mind that movement towards this initial commitment is a process that unfolds over time and that the process unfolds differently for different people.

Some people are invited into the life of a vital congregation where over time they are able to consider the

Gospel and make a commitment. Others refuse to have anything to do with church, but as the Gospel is explained to them, clearly and patiently, they make the decision to follow Jesus, and eventually come into the church. Either way, over time, there are several issues that you might well expect to be part of your conversation.

Your Church

Almost inevitably you will talk about your church. For many of us, the invitation to a friend or acquaintance to accompany us to a worship service will be our first practical step in evangelism. In perhaps its purest form, evangelism is simply saying, "Come and see." Come with me to our church and see who we are, how we live, what we do. Experience our community, learn about God's grace, and see if all of this has any attraction for you.

It is surprising how many people are open to an invitation to go to church. Again and again in my ministry, I meet people who have somehow drifted away from church and who are willing to come back and give it another try. There are many people around us who are curious about faith but who have no idea how to go about finding and attending a church. Many of today's adults have little or no experience of church. Many of them are open, but they need our help.

Others are not so open, and it will take some time and effort to persuade them. Here, it is essential that you have thought out beforehand exactly what it is about your church that makes it so important to you, and why you think it would be beneficial for your friend to try it out. This form of evangelism, of course, requires the support of a loving, caring, teaching, healing, equipping community. We never achieve perfection in this, but we must constantly strive to make our congregations such places.

Your Story

You will also want to be prepared to share your personal faith story, as indicated in the previous chapter on witnessing. I would strongly encourage you to share this story with a Christian friend in order to become accustomed to telling it. If you can meet together with a group of Christians who are interested in evangelism, in order to share your faith stories with one another and to practise having these evangelizing conversations, so much the better.

In all my experience in evangelism I have never found anything to equal the power of a simple word of personal witness from someone willing to talk about how they came to faith and about what their faith means to them. Sharing your personal faith story is probably the most effective thing you can do in influencing another person towards Christ.

Remember that the basic question here is this: "What is the good news about Jesus which, from your personal experience, you would like to share?" Do not underestimate the power of your personal story. It might not seem particularly exciting to you, but people are not looking for excitement. They are looking for something to believe in, and they are looking for authenticity.

God's Story

We also indicated in the previous chapter that at some point you will want to be able to move beyond sharing your personal faith story in order to share something of God's story. God's story is so wide, so broad, so deep, so complex, that none of us will ever fully comprehend it in this lifetime. Discovering the vastness of this story is part of the adventure of lifelong discipleship. On the other hand, in order to influence people towards faith, we must be prepared to reduce this complexity to a simplicity that they are able to consider and reckon with. The following points, while certainly by no means exhaustive, cover what I believe are ten of the basic essentials needed by someone who wants to understand enough about the Christian faith to give it their serious and informed consideration. It might help increase your confidence in this area if you use these points to construct an outline or overview of God's story, to guide you as your evangelizing conversations unfold.

1. It is through Jesus that God is revealed to us. In Jesus we see God at work. Jesus models for us how God wants us to live and what is important to God.

2. Jesus came into the world in order to deal with evil. He came to set us free from the power of evil, to make provision for our sins, and to lead us back into friendship with God and into the life of God's kingdom.

3. Jesus was put to death, because evil wanted him out of the way — but he rose from the dead! It is through his death and resurrection that Jesus has rescued creation from the ultimate power of evil and death, and provided the means of forgiveness for the sins of the world.

4. Having risen from the dead, Jesus is alive — today and forever.

5. Jesus knows us intimately, inside and out, and loves us beyond our ability to imagine. The cross is one demonstration of this love.

6. Jesus stands ready to forgive us for all the things that have kept us from God and from the life of God's kingdom. He offers us a totally new beginning. *Jesus offers a totally new beginning!*

7. Jesus invites us to follow him, and to join him in the life and work of God's kingdom. In extending this invitation, he is perfectly aware of our past, our flaws,

and our failures, but he is more interested in our potential than in our weakness, in our future more than in our past.

8. This offer of forgiveness and new life is open to everyone. It is not made on the basis of merit. It cannot be earned. It is offered as a free gift to anyone who will accept it. This is what is meant by grace.

9. When we become followers of Jesus, we also become a part of his church. In the church we learn together what it means to be the people of God.

10. In trusting and following Jesus, we find eternal life. Death does not have the last word in God's kingdom. Jesus will lead us through death to resurrection in God's eternal kingdom.

These ten points, in my opinion, spell out in accessible fashion what it means to trust Jesus as Saviour and to follow him as Lord within the fellowship of his church. Remember, the point of this outline is not to help people qualify for a certificate in theology. The goal is to give them a clear enough grasp of what it means to follow Jesus that they will be able to give the matter serious and informed consideration.

CHAPTER EIGHT

How Should I Say It?

So far, we have just looked at the kinds of things you will want to say when engaged in a conversation about Jesus. But what is it like to be right on the spot? What personal dynamics can you expect? How should you begin, continue, and end the conversation? What if you are nervous?

I don't know if we can ever completely disarm the initial apprehension and reluctance many of us feel when we think about initiating an evangelizing conversation. We noted in an earlier chapter that the reasons for this initial reluctance and apprehension are varied and complex. For many of us, we will just have to accept that these feelings are to be expected, to name them, and to resolve that we will not let them keep us from realizing our desire to be faithful witnesses for Christ.

That said, however, the fact that we have been praying for guidance, and for discernment and courage, should go a long way towards overcoming our natural reluctance. Remember, we are not talking here about going door to door making cold calls, or seeking to engage total strangers on the street in life-changing conversations. We are talking about initiating a conversation with someone we know; with someone whose name has particularly stood out for us as we prayed for guidance over a number of names, and with someone for whom we are now praying on a daily basis that God will prepare their hearts for such a conversation, that we will be sensitive in discerning the right time for such a conversation, that we will have the courage to initiate such a conversation, and that

God will help us throughout the course of the conversation.

Keep in mind that seeking to influence someone towards faith in Christ is an act of genuine friendship. We wouldn't even be bothering with evangelism if we weren't convinced that helping someone turn to Christ would be a benefit to them. Everyone deserves to know how much God loves them and what Christ has done for them. Everyone deserves the chance to learn about the new life of God's kingdom to which they are invited. Why should people have to wait to hear this news from a stranger when they can hear it from a friend? Our desire to help people discover God's love and to become followers of Jesus is not selfish or self-serving. On the contrary, it is an indication of genuine friendship.

Knowing that we are engaged in an act of friendship should help make our evangelizing conversations as natural as possible. Nevertheless, it is helpful to have at least a broad outline of what such a conversation entails. This will help us keep our bearings and stay focused as we proceed through the conversation. It should also help to increase our confidence. The following outline describes what I believe to be the five essential components of a well-focused evangelizing conversation. (I am indebted to my friend, the Reverend David Mansfield, Director of Evangelism for the Anglican Diocese of Sydney, Australia, who identified these components for us in a workshop on evangelism training at Trinity Church, Streetsville, in June 1995.)

It is important to keep in mind that not all of these elements will be present in every conversation. However, taken together, they provide a helpful overview of what such a conversation entails, and by keeping this outline in mind, you will have a clear sense of what point you have reached and of what remains to be done in future exchanges.

1. Bridging

The most important part of any evangelizing conversation is simply getting it started. This is often not as difficult as we might fear. In fact, I am convinced that one of the keys to intentionally initiating faith-related conversations is just to stop deliberately ignoring the natural opportunities that regularly come our way!

My experience as a priest who seeks to encourage his congregation to think in terms of evangelism is that people often intentionally pass up clear opportunities, because they fear that the other person might feel uncomfortable. Well, sensitivity and consideration are certainly laudable, but we need to reassure ourselves that faith-related conversations are perfectly normal and natural. If our faith is important to us, it is only natural that we should want to talk about it. People understand that. They won't be shocked.

When you have a person's name on your Operation Andrew list and are praying on a daily basis for opportunities to have a faith-related conversation with that person, it stands to reason that whenever you are with that person, you will be on the alert for opportunities to guide the conversation in that direction. In fact, you will be thinking about how you can take the initiative in creating such opportunities.

Some opportunities are ready-made. Someone with whom you enjoy a healthy relationship, or with whom you are cultivating a friendship, might make a comment about the church or about Christianity or about another person's faith or about something in the news relating to religion. With a bit of thought, you can use such openings to make a preliminary statement about the fact that you are a Christian, and how you see the issue from that perspective. Then wait for the response. There might be a wonderful conversation just around the corner.

Sometimes the person might decide to confide in you about something that is troubling them. This often creates an opportunity to talk about where we find guidance, or about the difference a faith perspective can make in such a situation. Who knows where such an initiative might lead? It could turn out to be very exciting.

Sometimes, we will want to be proactive in directing the conversation in order to create an opportunity. In our culture, sometimes the mere mention of the fact that we attend church is enough to do the trick. Why not try making a point of learning to talk quite naturally with your friends about the fact that you attend church on Sundays? Make it a part of your conversation, just as you would about anything else that is important to you. Ask them what kind of a weekend they had. If they return the favour by inquiring about your weekend, make a point of telling them that you went to church. Say something like "And of course, we went to church on Sunday morning. That's an important thing in our family." Or, if you happen to be reading a Christian book, why not tell them about it? Or place it where they can notice it and maybe ask about it. Why not let them see this book on evangelism? That should be enough to get some kind of a conversation going!

The most appropriate bridge, of course, will depend to a large extent on the circumstances of the conversation and your personal knowledge of the person with whom you are talking. Building such bridges is probably more an art than a science, but with a bit of thought and some earnest prayer, combined with some practice and practical experience, we could all get better at it. The goal here is to get to the point where we can build these bridges naturally, sensitively, and unobtrusively.

2. Diagnosis

This stage has more to do with listening than with speaking. It should go without saying that listening is an essential part of effective evangelism. Listening shows that we take people seriously, that we are truly interested in who they are and in what is important to them. Everything in evangelism, from integrity to effectiveness, depends on our willingness to listen carefully and sensitively. Generally, our efforts to influence others towards choosing Jesus and the life of God's kingdom will only be as effective as our willingness to listen to their story.

The people with whom we seek to have faith-related conversations will be at different starting points in terms of understanding and openness. In this part of the conversation, we seek to discover how open they are to having such a conversation and what some of the issues will be as the conversation takes place. For example, does this person understand the claims of Christianity or will this be the first time they have heard the story of Jesus? Are they spiritually hungry and curious or are they cynical and embittered towards the Church? We should never make assumptions about these things.

Diagnosis usually begins with a question. Having mentioned that you go to church, for example, you might ask, "Do you go to church anywhere?" or if you know for a fact that they don't, you could say, "Have you ever been involved in a church?" This question should become second nature to anyone interested in influencing others towards Jesus. We should learn to ask this question as readily and as easily as we ask someone if they would like to join us for coffee. At any rate, the point of diagnosis is to discover the person's openness to the conversation, and to find out, in light of their background and attitude, what an appropriate starting point might be.

Sometimes the diagnosis will be a surprise, either positive or negative. You might find that this person is totally
open, that they have been wondering about spiritual issues for some time now, and wondering where they could
find some answers. I remember a woman coming to our
church a couple of years ago who said that she had been
looking for someone for two years who could tell her how
she could become a Christian. No one in her office was
able to help her; none of her friends seemed to know;
finally, someone recommended she come to our church.
This woman was totally open. Anyone seeking to start a
faith conversation with her would have been greatly encouraged. (Yes, she did become a Christian, and within a
few months of coming to our church, she was baptized.)

Sometimes we might be taken aback by a person's
hostility or reluctance. Many people are deeply fearful of
religion and faith. Others carry resentment towards the
church because of abuses in their past, real or imagined.
Obviously, this hostility will need to be addressed before
much progress can be made.

More than once in an evangelism workshop people
have told me about friends from whom they receive an
enraged or vitriolic response whenever the subject of
church or Christianity is raised. As a result, they are rather
reluctant to raise these subjects and prefer instead to skate
around them. But surely there are issues behind such a
response that it would be good to explore. Wouldn't a
friendship permit some gentle questioning about where
such a response comes from?

"I can't help but feel your anger towards the Church, or
towards God," you might say. "Have you been hurt by the
Church, or by Christian people at some point? Has God
disappointed you in some way? I'd really be interested in
hearing where you are coming from if you ever feel like
talking about it with me." Who knows what possibilities
such a conversation might hold?

3. Permission

Before we begin a serious evangelizing conversation, it is only courteous to ask permission. Asking permission is a relatively simple matter, and once granted, opens the door to a fruitful conversation. On the other hand, failure to ask permission is one of the reasons that evangelism frequently suffers from a bad reputation.

There are certain issues and areas of conversation which, in our culture, are considered to be personal and private. Issues relating to one's faith or spiritual beliefs are often regarded in this way. This does not mean that they shouldn't be talked about, but it does mean that you might be considered brash or insensitive if you just wade right into the conversation without asking permission. So much reluctance about evangelism stems from memories of uncomfortable experiences in which we felt cornered into having a conversation we didn't wish to have, and from our desire not to force that same experience onto someone else. Asking permission sets a more gracious climate. It disarms a lot of possible resentment and lends a certain dignity to the conversation.

It only takes a moment to ask permission. One or two sentences will do. For example, if in your bridging conversation you have mentioned that you went to church on Sunday, and if in your diagnostic question you have discovered that this person has long ago given up on the Church as irrelevant and boring, you might say something like, "I felt like that too until we discovered the church we attend now. We really enjoy it. I'd love to be able to tell you about it sometime if you're interested." Or perhaps, in response to a diagnostic question, your friend has indicated that she "has a lot of questions about religion." You might respond by saying, "Well, I'm certainly no theologian or biblical scholar, but my faith is very important to me and I would love to share with you what I'm learning about Jesus. Would you be open to that?"

I offer these simple examples just to give an idea of what I mean by asking permission. You will know best what is appropriate in your own particular situations. The important thing to remember is that the simple act of asking permission can disarm intimidation up front and pave the way to a relaxed and non-threatening conversation.

4. Making Your Case

Everything to this point has been by way of preparation, in order to bring you to the place in the conversation where you are able to present your case, or to make your point. Chances are that you haven't got to this point in the first two or three minutes. In fact, it might have taken six months or a year to get here. The bridging and diagnostic stages might last only a minute; on the other hand, either one of them might take several months. Similarly, it might take a long time before you are granted permission to make your case. But don't get discouraged. Remember, the Christian life is a marathon, not a sprint, and effective evangelism frequently takes time. Keep in mind that conversion is a process in which your part is simply to be a faithful and intentional witness. The results are up to God. Keep praying, stay on the alert, and see what happens.

What happens during this stage of the conversation (remember that this stage too will probably take place over an extended period of time) differs according to the individual circumstances of the people involved. Remember that your goal is to initiate a process through which you are seeking to influence this person to become a follower of Jesus.

Sometimes it will seem appropriate to invite the person to come to church with you right away. Sometimes it won't. A lot of ground may need to be covered before that can happen. In this case, you are probably going to spend a lot of time listening and responding to various questions and issues that are raised. In addition to sensitive listening, you will need to be willing to share what your faith means to you, and why it is important enough to you that you want to share it.

There are many different facets to the Gospel. As Geoffrey Willis points out in *Won by One*, the good news is like a Persian carpet made of many threads (p. 36). In addition to describing the aspect of the Good News that has most profoundly affected you, over time you will want to learn to talk about the part that might be most appropriate to the person with whom you are sharing. This is where it will be important to have in mind an overview of some of the essential features of God's story, as indicated above.

For some people, the promise of forgiveness for sins has magnetic power because they are going through life weighed down by guilt. Others will resonate more readily with the vision of working for God's kingdom, either because they are haunted by the apparent meaninglessness of life or because they have a deep-seated passion for justice. For some, the initial attraction will be the sense of community to be found amongst the people of God, while others, deeply conscious of their own mortality and perhaps frightened by the prospect of death, will be drawn by the promise of eternal life. Those who feel themselves of little value might well find themselves astonished at the revelation of God's grace and be completely overwhelmed at the realization of God's love for them.

No one presentation of the Gospel could possibly express all that it has to offer. Sensitive witnesses seek to share the aspects that have meant most to them personally, as well as the parts that they believe are most relevant to the friend with whom they are sharing.

5. Closure

I need to emphasize once more the importance of thinking about our faith-sharing conversations as "conversations in progress." Usually, they will unfold over time, in various situations and circumstances, each new conversation building on previous ones as trust is built and we are able to move more and more deeply into the conversation, both speaking and listening. As each episode of this conversation in progress draws to a close, a good closure will ensure that the conversation can continue at an appropriate time.

David Mansfield says that the best form of closure is to keep the conversation open. For example, you might close by saying, "I really enjoyed this conversation, especially hearing your memories of that church you attended as a child. Could we continue this conversation another time?" Or you might say, "I have really appreciated this conversation. Thanks for being so open with me and sharing your true feelings about religion. I would love to continue this conversation another time . . . would that be all right with you?" The goal here is to bring closure to the current conversation, while keeping the door open to continuing the conversation in the future.

What If It Works?

One of the most exciting things about witnessing is that it frequently turns out that, at some point, the person you have been working with and praying for indicates a readiness and openness to turn to Christ. This is exciting, but it shouldn't be surprising. This is someone for whom you have been praying, with whom you have been patiently modelling and sharing the Christian life. God has been working in this person's life, and now, by the mysterious working of God's Spirit, another heart is being opened to grace. So what do we do when someone is ready to become a follower of Jesus?

Introducing People to Jesus

In his book *Church Growth and the Power of Evangelism*, the Anglican priest and teacher Howard Hanchey describes evangelism as the ministry of introductions. I love this description. If the goal of evangelism is to encourage people to become followers of Jesus and to learn to live the life of God's kingdom, then evangelism is rightly seen as the ministry of introducing people to Jesus.

The Australian Anglican evangelist John Chapman, who for many years was Director of Evangelism for the Diocese of Sydney, relates the story of his embarrassment, as a young man, when a friend asked him if he could help him become a Christian. John had to tell his friend that he couldn't help him, but that fortunately he knew someone who could. He then called on another Christian friend to come and help. This Christian friend arrived and after a short conversation led the inquirer in a prayer of commitment to Christ. Chapman tells this story to make the point that he resolved there and then never to be in that situation again. He quickly learned how to introduce an inquirer to Jesus.

If we had guests in our house and another friend came to the door, we all would know how to introduce our friends to each other. As those who have committed ourselves to follow Jesus and to learn to live the life of God's kingdom, it is important that we learn how to introduce people to Jesus too.

I have long been convinced that when someone understands that Jesus is inviting him or her to follow him, and has come to the point of sincerely wishing to do so, the simple word *yes* is a perfectly adequate response. Spoken in response to the invitation of Jesus, "yes" is the most eloquent and powerful prayer in all the world. In church services in my congregation, I frequently invite those who are ready to turn to Christ to pray this one-word prayer — to simply say "yes" to Jesus.

Sometimes it seems more appropriate to say a longer prayer that spells out in more detail the commitment that is being made. I think of this as a parallel to wedding vows, where the precise nature of the commitment is spelled out, marking the moment of commitment and giving the couple a fixed point in their history where this commitment has been made to which they can occasionally return to get their bearings, and to which they can always look back with fondness and pleasure.

When a friend indicates a readiness to turn to Christ, the following prayer might provide a helpful model to follow:

Jesus, I realize that you already know me and that you love me. Now I want to get to know you too. Please forgive me for everything in my life that comes between us, and help me to renounce it as I learn to live the life of God's kingdom. Help me to follow you faithfully, and to grow to love you more and more. Amen.

Following the analogy of wedding vows, the "amen" in this prayer is the equivalent to the marriage ceremony's "this is my solemn vow" or "thereto I plight thee my troth."

Give your friend time to read this prayer carefully. Ask him if he understands it. Ask her if this prayer expresses what she wants to say to Jesus. Ask if they would like to say this prayer while you are there with them, or if they would like to take it home and pray it privately. Ask them to call you and let you know when they have prayed it. Praying this prayer with a friend whom we have helped influence to become a follower of Jesus is one of the great thrills of the Christian life. I wish this joy could be experienced by everyone who reads this book and by every Christian in your church. But be warned: The thrill of introducing a person to Jesus is addictive. When you have done it once, you can never get enough!

I am aware that there is a certain scandal of simplicity involved in all of this. "How simplistic!", we might be tempted to think. "To do something this simple would be an affront to the intelligence of anyone I know." Let me caution you about this. The temptation of the Church in evangelism today is not of making things too simple, but of making them too complex. In evangelism we are trying to make the very core of the faith accessible so that people can decide "yes" or "no." There is plenty of time ahead for learning and growth. Let's help people to get started first.

It just might turn out that someone you lead to Christ eventually decides to go on and get a Ph.D. in theology or biblical studies. That would be great! But that's for later. Right now, just keep it simple. And you will be amazed, in the course of your faithful witness, that the Gospel of Christ is nothing to be ashamed of. It is still, in the words of St Paul from almost two millennia ago, "the power of God for salvation to everyone who has faith" (Romans 1:16). Modern, educated, sophisticated people, hearing this message in its simplest form, still turn to Christ today, and in turning are converted and given new life! I know that this is true. I know because I see it happen in our church on a regular basis and I know that it happens in many other places as well.

This is my prayer for everyone who reads this book, and for every congregation that uses it as a guide in thinking about evangelism: that you will have the joy of influencing many within your spheres of activity to become followers of Jesus, and that you will see them grow to maturity and effective ministry within the fellowship of your church. They will thank you, you will be blessed, and there will be great rejoicing in heaven!

Suggestions for Further Reading

William Abrahams. *The Logic of Evangelism*. Nashville: Abingdon, 1989.

Walter Brueggemann. *Biblical Perspective on Evangelism*. Nashville: Abingdon, 1993.

Michael Green. *Evangelism through the Local Church*. London: Hodder & Stoughton, 1990.

Michael Green. *How Can I Lead a Friend to Christ?* London: Hodder & Stoughton, 1995.

Howard Hanchey. *Church Growth and the Power of Evangelism*. Cambridge, Mass.: Cowley, 1990.

Michael Marshall. *The Gospel Connection*. Harrisburg, Pa., Morehouse, 1990.

Donald Posterski. *Reinventing Evangelism*. Markham, Ont.: IVP, 1989.

Geoffrey Willis. *Won by One*. London: Marshall Pickering, 1994.

Study Guide

CHAPTER ONE: WHAT'S ALL THE FUSS?

1. What do you think Jesus means when he says, "The last will be first, and the first last"?

   The Lord loves losers
   There's more to life than winning or losing
   God helps those who can't help themselves
   God's standards for success are different from ours

   In your own life, have you experienced more successes, more failures, or about the same number of both? As you look back, which would you say has made you more open to God: the experience of "winning" or the experience of "losing"?

2. As you think of your church or your immediate circle of friends, which of the following do you think people would say they needed most in life?

   purpose and direction
   wholeness and healing
   companionship and community
   hope for transcendence or significance
   forgiveness
   reassurance about death

   Now imagine that you could be God for a day. What would you say to each of these friends?

3. *Group Discussion*

In different ways, Exodus 34:6–7, Luke 6:35–36, and Luke 15:11–32 each describe the character and characteristics of God. After reading all three passages, discuss the following questions:

a. Which of the divine characteristics described in the first two passages are best illustrated by the parable of the Prodigal Son?

b. If the father in the parable reflects God's priorities, in what way does his outlook differ from the expectations of the returning son? The attitude of the elder brother? Can you see any similarities between the attitudes and expectations of the two brothers and popular opinions about God today?

c. In your own experience, which of these divine characteristics most clearly represents "Good News" for your situation?

CHAPTER TWO: WHAT'S THE GOOD NEWS?

1. Imagine that your assignment is to explain to a good friend the role of Christ in resolving the estrangement between humanity and God. In terms of the modern professions that specialize in renegotiating broken relationships, does Christ's accomplishment most resemble that of

a criminal lawyer?
a government arbitrator in a labour dispute?
a marriage counsellor?
a diplomat or foreign minister?

Read 2 Corinthians 5:17–21.

2. In comparison to human relationships, what new risks and new responsibilities do God and the followers of Jesus each undertake at the different stages of their own relationship:

   passing acquaintance?
   firm friendship?
   mutual commitment and intimacy?

   Given the risks and responsibilities that are appropriate to each new stage, what suggestions or practical assistance could you provide to someone who asked for help in deepening their relationship with God? In overcoming their fear of God? In asking tough questions of God?

3. *Group Discussion*

   According to Revelation 21:3–4, the ultimate Good News is that under God's reign there will be no more tears or sorrows, sickness or death. In light of Jesus' own triumph over sin and death, to what degree does this Good News affect our lives now, and to what extent does its effect remain in the future? As we share this Good News with other people, what can we say that God provides in the present, and how much remains a promise?

CHAPTER THREE: YOU'RE INVITED: R.S.V.P.

1. If the Good News requires a response, imagine that your job is to issue the invitations. To help you decide on the wording of each invitation, consider first whether you and Jesus are summoning people to

attend a wedding feast
get involved in local politics
join a wake
view a dramatic presentation
invest in a business venture
undertake a dangerous mission
claim a grand prize
appear in court
contribute to a charity
start a neighbourhood improvement project
play on a sports team

What other information should be included? Is there any "fine print," or hidden cost? What should the invitees bring? Is attendance by personal invitation only, or can others come along?

2. If evangelism consists of three doors, labeled "Child of God," "People of God," and "Reign of God" (the individual, corporate, and public dimensions of Christian discipleship, respectively), which access point do you feel most familiar with, and which would you feel most comfortable inviting someone else to enter? In your own words, what do you understand to lie on the other side of each of these three doors?

3. *Group Discussion*

Compile a list of all the different strategies you have ever tried in order to get someone else (children, spouse, colleagues, rivals) to agree with you or say "yes," and all the different tricks and techniques that others have tried on you. (This question will be made easier by having (a) salespeople and (b) a good sense of humour, in your group.) Next, list the advantages and disadvantages of each method, and try to decide which (if any) are legitimate means for helping people say "yes" to God.

CHAPTER FOUR: UNDERSTANDING RELUCTANCE

1. Reviewing the content of this chapter, try to formulate a positive principle or guideline for evangelism that corresponds to each "Reason for Reluctance":

   Charlatans   Cynicism
   Unwelcome Intrusions   The Condition of the
   Religious Fanatics   Church
   Self-Interest   Lack of Confidence in
   Empire Building   Ourselves
   Relativism   Lack of Confidence in
                                   the Gospel

2. If evangelism is like *The Wizard of Oz*, which of the following characters (and their needs) can you identify with?

   The Tin Man (who needs a heart [compassion])
   The Scarecrow (who needs a brain [understanding])
   The Lion (who needs courage)
   Dorothy (who needs a home and a family)

   Which of these needs can be supplied by your companions on the journey, and which can come only as gift from the throne in the City?

3. *Group Discussion*

   If you were to compare the Church (as you know and have experienced it) to the people of God as they make their way toward the Promised Land, which of the following would best describe your situation?

   still in bondage
   set free from captivity; experiencing God's deliverance
   being led, fed, and strengthened in the desert

spying out the Promised Land; intimidated by its
   challenges
wandering in the wilderness
crossing the Jordan River
taking possession of God's gifts
at rest in the place of promise

In your estimation, what does the Church need most
to help it enter into (or at least draw closer to) its
spiritual inheritance? At what stage can other travellers
be invited to join this journey of faith?

CHAPTER FIVE: THE CONGREGATIONS WE NEED

1. As you think about your own church, reflect on the
   "Three Key Questions" outlined in this chapter:

   a. What would we like to see happen in the lives of the
      people who come to join in the life of this congre-
      gation? What resources or activities are required (or
      are already in place) to bring about such a result?

   b. What, from the point of view of those we would like
      to reach, would make this church a worthwhile
      community to join? How do non-members view our
      congregation and ministry?

   c. What price are we as a congregation prepared to pay
      in order to reach and assimilate newcomers? What
      price are we *not* willing to pay?

2. Try to envisage your church as though it were a small
   business or service agency. Then try to answer the
   following questions:

a. What is your main "product" or service, and to whom is it provided?

b. Are members of the congregation producers and service providers, or primarily consumers?

c. What is the role of management, and how effectively is that role performed?

d. Where can this church find, and how can it best attract, new "customers," clients, or consumers?

After careful analysis, design a plan or strategy for the next one, three, or five years, aimed at ensuring the long-term viability and effectiveness of this Christian "enterprise."

3. *Group Discussion*

Which of the "Five Key Areas of Congregational Life" does your church presently need to address in order to help it move from "maintenance" to "mission"?

Transformational Leadership
The Ministry of Making Disciples
Becoming a Community
Giving Pastoral Care Back to the People
Developing Celebratory Worship

In each of the areas you have identified, try to compose brief job descriptions for the parish leaders, the congregation as a whole, and the individual members to help the church bring about the desired change.

CHAPTER SIX: MY ROLE IN EVANGELISM

1. In your own spiritual life, would you say that God came looking for you, that you went looking for God, or both? What would you say to someone who asked you to relate the most astonishing thing that God, or Christ, has ever done for you?

2. As you consider your own role in influencing others towards Jesus, would your personal experience and abilities be most helpful to someone who was:

   considering the possibility of Christian faith (1–48 on Bowen's scale)?
   interested in exploring Christian commitment (49–51)?
   seeking to grow in Christian discipleship (52 onwards)?

   Who do you know that fits the description you have selected?

3. *Group Discussion*

   Take turns in your group practising your "story-telling" skills, by listening graciously and helping each other to recount:

   a. God's Story (the biblical account of God's involvement in human history, and especially the story of Jesus); and

   b. Your Story (the influences, turning points, and significant features of your faith journey, together with what following Jesus means for you today).

Chapter Seven: Getting Started

1. Draw three circles on a piece of paper and label them "Family," "Work," and "Neighbourhood." Inside each circle, carefully, thoughtfully, and prayerfully list the names of the people with whom you have regular contact within that sphere of influence. Pray for these individuals over the next week, asking God to enrich their spiritual lives and to show you which of them would be most responsive to a conversation about Christian faith. At the end of the week, answer the following questions:

   a. Which individuals have come repeatedly to mind, or for whom have you sensed a particular need to pray?

   b. What are some of the ways that you could, over time, get to know these individuals better, demonstrate friendship, or deepen the level of trust between you?

   c. What specific benefit would you like to see in these individuals' lives as a result of their becoming followers of Jesus?

2. On a second piece of paper, make a list of all the different factors that influenced you to join the Church, to consider trusting God, or to want to contribute to the work of God's kingdom. Of all your family members, friends, and colleagues, with whom do you have a similar influence, and in what way might you be able to exercise that influence in a more gracious or effective manner?

3. *Group Discussion*

   Choose one of the following questions and share your answer either aloud (3 minutes maximum) or in written form (150 words or less):

   a. What would you lose if you were never again permitted to attend church or to meet with other Christians?

   b. What finally convinced you that God, or Christ, was real, and able to make a difference to your life?

   c. What is your favourite story from the Bible, and what does it tell you about God?

CHAPTER EIGHT: HOW SHOULD I SAY IT?

1. Think of your best friend, your worst enemy, and the person you admire most: review in your mind everything you know about these three individuals. After prayer and careful consideration, answer the following questions:

   a. If each of them were to ask, "Where do you think God is at work in *my* life?" what would you say?

   b. If God were to grant you one wish for each of them, what would you ask for?

   If you are unable to answer either question because you do not know the person well enough, what could you do to learn more about them?

2. With the help of a friend (or a mirror, if you prefer!), role-play the different elements of an evangelizing conversation:

Bridging	Making Your Case
Diagnosis	Closure
Permission	

   Imagine yourself on the receiving end of your own conversation. Which parts seem most natural? Most awkward? What factors might contribute to or detract from the integrity, sensitivity, and graciousness of such a conversation?

3. *Group Discussion*

Either aloud, or using slips of paper, have each person in your group list the following:

a. Your greatest difficulty in sharing your faith, or introducing others to Jesus.

b. Your greatest strength, asset, or ability as it applies to sharing the Good News of Jesus.

c. The most helpful encouragement or practical assistance that you could provide to someone engaged in the ministry of evangelism.

Try to match as many "assets" and "liabilities" as possible within your group, in order for you to help one another with this aspect of Christian discipleship. Conclude your meeting by praying for one another, according to the strengths and needs of each.